# KAFFE FASSETT
## *Glorious Knitting*

# KAFFE FASSETT
## *Glorious Knitting*

# *Photography by*
# *Steve Lovi*

EBURY PRESS · LONDON

Editor/Sandy Carr
Design/Gillian Allan
Assistant to Kaffe Fassett/Zoë Hunt
Pattern checker/Marilyn Wilson
Charts/Dennis Hawkins
Additional artwork/Coral Mula

First published in 1985 by Century
Published in 1992 by Ebury Press
an imprint of Random House UK Ltd
Random House
20 Vauxhall Bridge Road
London SW1V 2SA

Reprinted 1985 (twice), 1986 (twice), 1987, 1988 (twice), 1989 (twice)

A catalogue record for this book is available from the British Library.

ISBN 0-09-177670-8 (Paperback)

Phototypeset by Rowland Phototypesetting Ltd
Bury St Edmunds, Suffolk
Colour origination by Newsele srl (UK), Milan
Printed in Portugal by
Printer Portuguesa Lda, Lisbon
D.L.B. 22336-1985

Note: *the garments on the title page and opposite
the title page are the Large Step Jacket (page 54)
and the Toothed Stripe Waistcoat (page 37).*

# CONTENTS

* Yarn packs are obtainable for these patterns. See page 158 for information.

# INTRODUCTION

Like many other crafts, knitting has the potential to create magic in our lives. Mosaic-making, woodcarving, tapestry, quilting and so on, are all capable of lifting everyday household objects out of the ordinary to brighten up our days. Instead, they are often responsible for drab, uninspired works that have the opposite effect. In my teaching workshops I try to persuade people that they can make something really beautiful and life-enhancing and I usually encounter the same protest, 'But you're an artist. You *know* about colour and we don't.' This misconception is one of the main reasons for my writing this book. I want to try to convey to you that a sense of colour is not something you automatically know about; you discover and rediscover its secrets by playing with it and, above all, by constantly *looking*. So as well as giving you some of my patterns in great detail, I particularly want to show you how these designs evolved—the experimenting with sources of inspiration for colours and shapes that is a never-ending process. The missionary in me fervently hopes you will pick up the challenge offered here to continue this creative train of thought into your own unique flights of fancy.

My own story in the knitting world is a graphic example of 'ignorance is bliss'. Having spent most of my life, until the age of 28, as a painter of still life and portraits, I had no experience of needlework.

*Inspiration can be drawn from many unexpected corners, for instance, this Victorian mosaic plate (for needlepoint) and a lichen-covered slate (for knitting).*

Often I would find myself drooling over some richly woven or embroidered cloth in a still life and wonder how on earth it was made. Now at that time, in the early sixties, there was a taboo against 'serious' artists dabbling in the crafts. However, on a fabric-buying trip with Bill Gibb to the Holm Mills in Inverness, I finally succumbed. The knitting yarns at the back of the mill were such exquisitely subtle colours that I could restrain myself no longer: I bought about twenty colours and some knitting needles on the spot.

All the way to the train I was planning to find a knitter whom I could direct to make the wonderful creations I knew these colours were capable of producing. How to plan it? What was possible? I knew so little about it and was sure it would all take far too long. Gradually it dawned on me that I must learn to knit, and design as I went along. Fortunately, travelling in our party was a good knitter who taught me to cast on, knit and purl, and I was away! By the time we reached London, I was hooked. The following weeks found me knitting from six in the morning. I put all twenty colours into that first cardigan (above).

Over the next few years I ignored many of the rules that seem to paralyse most knitters into sticking to monochrome garments. Merrily, I combined colours and textured yarns, made knots in the middle of rows, and used up to twenty colours in a single row in some of my more ambitious efforts. Playing with this most wonderful fabric I poured every influence I encountered into it—tiled floors, ancient walls, carpets, early maps were all turned into knitting designs.

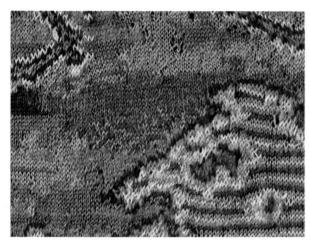

During the next fifteen years I collected yarns in wonderful colours and textures everywhere I travelled, but I always dreamed of producing my own colours. The invitation finally came with a call from Stephen Sheard of Rowan Yarns in Yorkshire. After I had chosen colours for cotton chenilles and wool tweeds, it became apparent that patterns were required for using them, hence my first knitting packs.

Many people were afraid that the 'average knitter' would not be able to cope with numerous colours and complex-looking graphs. I knew from my own experience that there was nothing to fear, so I began a series of lectures and workshops to spread the word! Sometimes in my weekend workshops the enthusiasm reaches fever pitch as 'the average knitter' tosses the rules out of the window and produces a glorious knitted 'poem' in twenty-five colours.

A great part of the success of these workshops and of my one-off designs in general is due to Zoë Hunt, who works out all my shapes and gives me the benefit of her skills and experience. Another partner in my work is weaver Richard Womersley, whose fine sense of colour is a constant help to me in my designs. Steve Lovi, whose sensitive eye is responsible for the photographs in this book, has also advised with great inspiration on many of the garments. For me it is a wonderful luxury to have constant help and feedback from such a perceptive and talented team.

We are all aware how complicated and demanding some of these designs may appear. Yet most knitters happily discover what an illusion this complexity is. Many of the designs have been successfully completed by quite inexperienced knitters. People often fear that they will not have the patience to finish a garment. Usually, however, when you see a colourful garment taking shape, the opposite is the case—the difficulty is to put it down! We all have a fundamental need to do something really well. If knitting with colours turns out to be your particular road to self-expression, then you will have started on a marvellously rewarding and adventurous journey.

(Far left) *I've used old maps as the source for a wide range of garments and furnishings. This one was made for an exhibition of miniature textiles in crewel wool on 2mm (US 0) needles.*

(Below) *I worked the tapestry hanging on the wall of my studio (left) from my favourite china pots. The chair covered in needlepoint was done for Designers Guild.*

# Knitting with Colours

Let's get one thing straight at the start. This is not a knitting pattern book in the usual sense. Although there are patterns, lots of them, I would be very disappointed if they were always followed word for word.

What I would really like to do is invite you to paint with wool. Having been a painter for years, I can tell you that needlework is a much more enjoyable way of working with colour than painting and requires far less instruction to get satisfying results. I'm assuming that you already have your basic knitting skills, which are, amazingly, all you need to create these designs.

## THEMES AND VARIATIONS

In each section of the book my intention is to create a map of inspiring ideas that, once grasped, will lead you into many adventurous side paths. I've taken themes (mostly geometric—circles, squares and so on) and explored just a few of the possible variations in several garments. But whatever ground I've covered is only the tip of a huge iceberg, the rest of which you can uncover for yourself.

Some limitations or rules can be stimulating and I set a few for myself. For me, knitting garments is about pattern not pictures. You can always make even a complex picture into a pattern by repeating or formalizing it—I've made patterns out of bowls of fruit, fans, flowers and more. But I don't feel that large pictorial sweaters are really flattering to wear (any rule has exceptions, of course).

My other rule is to follow through with a pattern. Nothing disappoints me more than a richly decorated front and the let-down of a solid one-colour back. I often put different patterns on the back of waistcoats, such as stripes that continue the colours round (see opposite).

I hope you will take the patterns in this book and play around with them. Some of them tell you exactly what colours to use and where. By all means use these patterns to give you the feel of using lots of colours. Others give you the garment shaping and pattern layout and you can decide for yourself what colours to use. In time I hope you will build on these ideas, changing pattern layouts as well as adding more colours—my motto is always, 'When in doubt, add twenty more colours'!

## ABOUT YARNS

The first thing you have to do when knitting with colours is clear your mind of some inhibiting preconceptions and prejudices that have built up over the years. For instance, I never worry about running out of yarn and mixing dye lots, and I often combine all sorts of yarns in the same garment.

When you're using twenty, thirty or more colours in a garment, the amount used of any one of them is usually quite small, often less than a 25g (1oz) ball. So you are unlikely to run out, but if you do and you cannot get the same dye lot, then this is a bonus—you may even have to combine two finer yarns to get a similar tone, and the effect will probably be delightful. It's just this sort of subtle variation that we are looking for.

Because only small amounts of any one colour are needed, many of the garments can be made up of odd balls of yarn left over from other projects or bought in markets and at sales. Try to build these up into a store of beautiful colours by buying a few balls of anything that takes your fancy. Buy a nucleus of inexpensive plain wools and add a few special luxury items as you go along—mohairs, silks and so on. I keep all my yarns separated by colour: I'll have one drawer for yellows, another for pinks, another for blues . . .

## YARN QUANTITIES

In patterns where the actual colours are specified, the amounts for each colour are also listed. That amount is never less than 25g (1oz) since it's usually impossible to buy in smaller quantities, so there will be lots left over and these can be added to your stockpile. If you do not wish to use the yarn specified, an equivalent thickness of yarn is given.

*'Liberty Bazaar', painted for a red room, is a typical example of the subject matter I use in my still life painting—oriental pots, embroideries and a Russian scarf all set against a Chinese silk robe. It shows how the use of several shades of a colour can create an exciting richness.*

In patterns where the actual colours are not specified, the overall quantity and thickness of yarn has been given, together with any other relevant information. The weights are only approximate, however, and will vary depending on exactly what type of yarn is chosen (cotton, wool, mohair and so on). The number of colours is also left up to you. Many of them could be worked in anything from five to fifty or sixty colours (or more).

The best advice I can give is to buy as much as you can whenever you can. If you have lots left over, so much the better—you'll have a wonderful palette of colours ready for that rainy day when the urge to begin a glorious new jacket becomes overwhelming.

## CHOOSING YARNS
When it comes to a choice between natural and man-made fibres, I always pick natural fibres whenever possible. So far I've not experienced a man-made fibre that breathes or retains its shape as well as wool. Sometimes, however, if I stumble across the most delectable shade in acrylic or synthetic mixtures, my inclination is to work it into the garment here and there. With careful washing it wears reasonably well. Even so, I keep man-mades to a small area, balanced out by many other yarns; all my garments are at least eighty per cent natural yarns.

Often I mix cotton and silk into predominantly woollen garments. Neither of these fibres gives as beautifully as wool (they are quite unsuitable for ribs, for example, as they aren't elastic enough), but they do give a crisp texture change that enhances a colour design.

Silk, especially, takes colour gorgeously and shines it back if polished, or glows with a matt depth if raw. I use it, like mohair, to lighten a garment that's getting heavy with chunky tweeds and thick cottons. Cotton is crisp and cool to wear and takes colour well. It can be hard to knit as it doesn't have the elasticity of wool. I tend to knit it loosely if colours are being carried across the back, as the fabric can be too stiff otherwise.

Mohair has a filmy lightness that can act like a glaze in painting, softening the effects of crisper yarns like wool and cotton.

## MIXING YARNS
I mix yarns in two different ways: I use several different textures in the same garment—mohair, chenille, silk, tweed, cotton, wool; also, I combine finer yarns and knit them as one, which enables me to get even more variation of tone and texture. If you want to do this, make sure you have a range of fine yarns in your stockpile. Of course, you must keep the overall thickness of yarns more or less even. For example, if the overall weight of your yarn is chunky (that is, the chunky yarns are used singly), then you can combine a mohair with a double knitting (knitting worsted) to go with it, or two double knittings, or a thin chenille with a double knitting.

## YARN PACKS
Yarn packs are obtainable for all those designs where the actual colours and types of yarn are specified. This will save you much shopping around for the exact colours as each pack will contain all the yarns listed in the materials section of the pattern. See page 158 for a list of packs and the addresses of suppliers.

## TENSION
I sympathize with knitters who are impatient to get on with the job and do not want to spend time on tension samples. However, the same instructions in the hands of tight or loose knitters can end up in a child's jacket or a huge coat. So the dreaded tension squares are absolutely essential if hours of work are not to be wasted.

You really must match your tension to that given in the patterns, so change the needle size until it is fully adjusted. Remember also that where the instructions give the tension 'over pattern', then the tension square must be worked from the chart and the colours handled as specified. Also, try to use several of the yarns specified (if any combinations are called for, make sure to work them in the tension sample).

Working tension samples need not be uncreative. For example, you could do each one in a different colour scheme and so try out colours at the same time. Save all the squares and sew them together into a blanket. I did this with lots of my first swatches and samples (see page 102), and now I have a superb sampler history of my early knitting life.

## HANDLING MANY COLOURS
Most of my patterns look infinitely complicated, rich and intricate, which tends to make people think they are extremely difficult to knit. In fact they are all well within the capabilities of the average knitter. I only ever use stocking stitch and ribs, with the occasional edging of crochet or garter stitch, so all you really have to think about are the colours.

Handling a large number of colours is something that worries quite a lot of knitters. In fact, it's not as difficult as it seems. Many of the patterns only use two or three colours to a row—it's just that those colours change frequently and that's what makes them seem complicated. The most important thing when knitting with lots of colours is to handle the yarns

*(Left) A side view of my first attempt at patterned knitting. This waistcoat shows my attraction to Celtic motifs and colours. After knitting the more ornate fronts, I followed the colours through with a simpler striped back and armhole edging.*

# Introduction

*The wrong sides of the Tumbling Blocks Crew-neck Sweater (page 76) and the Little Circles Sleeveless Pullover (page 136) show the two basic methods of handling many colours: intarsia (left), where the colours are knitted in place and knitting-in (right) where they are carried across the back of the work and either 'stranded' or woven in. The intarsia method creates a single thickness fabric whereas knitting-in creates a double or triple thickness depending on the number of colours in the row.*

properly. There are two main methods: intarsia and knitting-in.

**The intarsia method** (above left) is mostly used where there are lots of different colours in a row, many of them used in only one or two places. Instead of being carried across the back, these yarns are simply worked in their place then left hanging until the next row, and the next colour is knitted. In most cases, it is important to twist the two yarns together at the colour change to avoid holes (this is especially important when working vertical lines).

**Knitting-in** (above right) is really my term for what Fair Isle knitters call 'weaving in'. When two or more colours are used repeatedly in a row, the yarn not being worked is carried across the back until it is next needed. If only a few stitches are spanned, then it can simply be looped, or 'stranded', across (very loosely). If there are more than about five stitches to span, it should be woven under and over the working yarn as you go, so that the looped yarns are caught at the back of the work (I always operate these 'floating' yarns with my left hand). Some knitters knit-in in this way on every other stitch, but I find it sufficient to do it on every third stitch or so.

It is very important that the stranding or weaving is done at a relaxed even tension or the knitting will pucker. In any case, this method does pull in a great deal more than the intarsia method, and therefore results in quite a different tension, so it's vital not to get the two confused.

I also knit in all the ends of yarn as I work. This saves hours of laborious darning in after the knitting is over. It's basically the same as knitting in the floating yarns. What you do is this (see also below); when joining in a new colour leave ends of about 8cm (3in) on the old yarn and the new; work the next two stitches with the new yarn then, holding both ends in your left hand, lay them over the working yarn and work the next stitch; now insert the right-hand needle into the next stitch in the usual way, then bring the ends (still holding them in your left hand) up over the point of the right-hand needle and work this stitch past the ends. Carry on in this way laying the ends over the working yarn on every second or third stitch and knitting past the ends on the following stitch until they are completely knitted in.

WORKING WITH MANAGEABLE LENGTHS
This is the hottest tip for speed and the preservation of your sanity when knitting with many colours. The different yarns inevitably get tangled at the back of the work, so I rarely have balls or bobbins attached. Instead I break off short lengths of 60–100cm (2–3ft), depending on the area to be covered, and use these. As they get tangled it's easy just to pull through the colour you want. When more of a colour is required tie on another length, knitting in all the ends as you work. This method also encourages you to introduce subtle changes of tone.

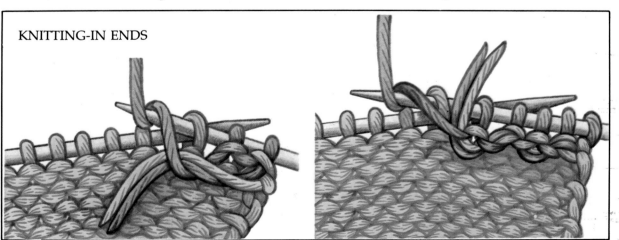

KNITTING-IN ENDS

## CIRCULAR NEEDLES

I almost always use circular needles (twinpins). Sometimes you have to use them (or double-pointed needles) for working neckbands in the round, but they are also much more convenient than the conventional pairs of straight needles even for flat knitting. When making garments in one piece (all the jackets and coats in this book are made this way), the knitting can get very heavy. With straight needles this weight is taken by your arms; with circular needles it rests much more comfortably in your lap. Circular needles can also hold far more stitches than straight needles.

## SWISS DARNING

Swiss darning (or duplicate stitch) is a great boon when knitting with colours. Any book on knitting techniques will tell you how to do it, but basically you simply cover a stitch or several stitches with yarn in a different colour after the knitting has been completed. This means that you can correct mistakes without having to unravel your work, you can add extra colours to give a scheme just a little more lift, and you can mask a colour that isn't working.

## READING THE PATTERNS

There are two types of pattern in this book: those where the actual colours are specified and those where they're not. In a way, the latter are easiest to follow; although you have to make more decisions of your own, you don't have to be constantly checking charts and colour sequence tables to see if you're using the right colours. In that sense, you can't go wrong, and if you want to work the other patterns in the same way, ignoring the colours I've specified, then, of course, you can do so. However, if you're nervous about choosing colours, or if you want something exactly like the garment pictured, then go for a pattern where the yarns are specified.

Sizes Where there are several sizes, these are listed in the measurements section of each pattern (standard measurement equivalents to metric, and US needle sizes are given in round brackets). The instructions for larger sizes, where they differ, are given in square brackets.

Charts Most of the patterns are worked from charts. Each square on a chart represents a stitch, and each row of squares a row of knitting. You read knit rows from right to left and purl rows from left to right (unless otherwise instructed); and you start at the bottom of the chart and work up (unless otherwise instructed).

The symbols on the chart refer to the colours or yarns to be used for those stitches. In some cases there will also be a colour sequence table or key to the symbols which will tell you exactly what colour to use for each stitch. In other cases, you follow the pattern layout but choose your own colours. Sometimes the chart for the whole garment is given; alternatively, only a section will be given and it may be necessary to repeat it several times. All this will be explained on the charts themselves or in the instructions.

Once you get used to them, charts are much easier to work from than written instructions because you can see exactly what you are supposed to be doing. Often the first few rows are written out just to get you started. To help keep your place, cover the part of the chart not yet worked with a piece of stiff card.

## FINISHING

Some things can make or break a garment as far as I'm concerned. Many of these are to do with the way it is finished. Working edgings too loosely or too tightly has, above all else, given hand knitting a bad name. After working an edging for the first time, we often find that we need more or fewer stitches and have to unpick and reknit it, so don't be afraid to redo them if they don't work out initially. These patterns tell you exactly how many stitches to pick up (for neckbands, collars and so on), but the essential thing is to space the stitches *evenly* along the appropriate edge.

Plain wide button and buttonhole bands are another of my *bête noires*. I like them to be patterned or striped or, if they have to be plain, as narrow as possible. This is why we always make our buttonholes on the same row as we pick up the stitches. Some of you may find this a bit tricky, in which case do make your buttonholes in the usual way, but add stripes or patterns to avoid that wide blank strip down the front of the garment. I like the buttons to all but disappear into a garment while still having a quiet life of their own, and I'm always combing markets to find special ones.

Good pressing also makes an enormous difference, especially to patterned knitting. Since I use mixtures of yarns I always play safe and press with a steam iron or over a damp cloth. I don't like to flatten the knitting completely so I try not to be too heavy-handed. We also pay special attention to pressing seams and hems.

---

ABBREVIATIONS
alt—alternate(ly)
approx—approximately
beg—begin(ning)
cm—centimetre(s)
cont—continu(e)(ing)
dec—decreas(e)(ing)
foll—follow(s)(ing)
g—gram(s)
in—inch(es)
inc—increas(e)(ing)
K—knit
K up—pick up and knit
mm—millimetres
oz—ounce(s)
P—purl
patt—pattern
rem—remain(s)(ing)
rep—repeat(s)
rs—right side of work
sl—slip
st(s)—stitch(es)
st st—stocking stitch (stockinette stitch)
tbl—through back of loop(s)
tog—together
ws—wrong side of work
yrn—yarn round needle (yarn over)

# STRIPES

Technically, the stripe is the easiest colour pattern to achieve in knitting. There are no changes of colour within the rows; you just knit one row, or two or twelve or whatever, in one colour at a time. Getting a really exciting use of colour, however, even with simple stripes, is one of the greatest challenges of all.

Stripes are the most basic textile pattern and every culture since time began has developed its own variations. Think of Japanese Kabuki costumes, African cottons, Arab rugs and robes, Indian blankets. Many of these were the inspiration for some of the rich variety of stripes you see in European furnishings and garments, from elegant French silks to grandad's striped pyjamas.

Stripes don't have to be dull: they can be as bold as brass or intricate and repeating. They can cut

you in bands horizontally or give you a feeling of length vertically. They can start simply as straight lines, then fragment into complex points like those in the Toothed Stripe patterns, or they can travel and bend in gentle waves until they become steps and zigzags. When you see them overlapping, as on a clothes line or a field of deck chairs, stripes can gain an interesting complexity. (It was this that inspired the Striped-patch designs on page 122.)

When designing stripe patterns it can help to wrap yarns round a strip of cardboard or folded paper. Pin the card on a wall so that you can see how the colours 'read' from a distance. Then knit up a swatch and live with it for a while before you commit yourself to a full-scale garment. I pin mine up opposite my bed, so I'll see it when I wake up in the morning (always a perceptive time for me).

If something isn't working it will become quite apparent.

The layout of the stripes can be just as important as the colours. Draw some outlines of the garment shape on a piece of paper and paint your stripes on them in different directions. Don't forget that if you knit the garment from cuff to cuff (like the Ikat sweater on page 30), vertical stripes become just as easy to knit as horizontal ones.

Words are hopelessly inadequate when dealing with the intensely visual subjects of colour and pattern. The best thing you can do always is to knit up lots of swatches. Even if you think you know what a colour will look like, do try it with several other colours and study them from a distance. Often, I find surprising new qualities in colours by trying combinations I was sure would be dull.

*I love overlapping stripes on lots of different scales. Here you can see bedspreads, carpets and lots of very simply striped sweaters in the background. You can experiment with stripes on any plain garment patterns but I've given you a very simple T-shirt to get you started (far right and on page 14). The T-shirt on the far left is a bold simplified version of the Jack's Back Stripe in cotton (you'll find others on pages 19–20). Next to it is another in a dotted stripe under a diagonal striped waistcoat. Then there's Zoë in the red Ikat Stripe Batwing (page 30) and a back view of my very first waistcoat.*

# Simple Stripes

This is the easiest possible introduction to knitting with colours—a basic T-shaped top, a gathered skirt and triangular shawl. There's very little shaping and no charts to worry about, so you can concentrate on the colours. With the top, which is knitted from side to side, you can work out your own stripe sequence or follow the one given in the pattern row for row, if that's what you want. With the skirt and shawl (see page 16), however, you have to start making your own decisions—you are given the shapes but you can put the stripes wherever you like.

## Striped T-shirt

This is knitted from side to side in fine cotton chenille for the most part, with touches of plain wool and fine tweed. The colours specified in the pattern are those of the red version (below). The sleeves are elbow length, but you can easily make them shorter by working fewer rows on the left sleeve before casting on for the body, and working the same number of rows before casting off on the right sleeve. To make longer sleeves, work more rows on each one.

### MATERIALS
**Yarn used**
50[75,100]g (2[3,4]oz) Rowan Yarns Fine Cotton Chenille each in cyclamen 385 (C) and cardinal 379 (N); 50g (2oz) each in mole 380 (M) and lacquer 388 (Q); 25g (1oz) each in plum 386 (A), black 377 (B), steel 382 (E), carnation 389 (F), shark 378 (H), bran 381 (R), seville 387 (S), turquoise 383 (T) and purple 384 (U)
50g (2oz) Rowan Yarns Double Knitting Wool in black 62 (V); 25g (1oz) each in orange/brown 78 (D), green/brown 407 (G) and bright pink 95 (J)
25g (1oz) Rowan Yarns Light Tweed in lavender 213 (L)
**Equivalent yarn** double knitting
1 pair each 3mm (US 2) and 3¾mm (US 5) needles
1 set four double-pointed 3mm (US 2) needles (or circular needle)

### TENSION
17 sts and 27 rows to 10cm (4in) over st st on 3¾mm (US 5) needles.

### MEASUREMENTS
**To fit bust/chest** 86[91,96]cm (34[36,38]in)
**Actual width** 91[97,101]cm (36[38,40]in)
**Length to shoulder** 54cm (21in)
**Side seam** 26cm (10in)
**Sleeve seam** 34cm (13½in)

### BACK, FRONT AND SLEEVES (one piece)
Beg at left cuff, using 3mm (US 2) needles and yarn V, cast on 95 sts.
Work 16 rows st st, beg with a K row.
K 2 rows to form foldline.
Change to 3¾mm (US 5) needles and cont in st st stripes, foll colour sequence table, for 91 rows.
**Shape back and front**
Cast on 45 sts at beg of next 2 rows. 185 sts.
Cont in patt, work 21 [25,29] rows.
**Divide for neck**
Next row Patt 93 sts, turn, leaving rem sts on a spare needle and cont on these sts only for back. Work 80 rows, leave these sts on a spare needle and rejoin yarn to sts left on first spare needle. Work 81 rows.
**Next row** Patt across sts on both needles to join back and front. 185 sts.
Work 21 [25,29] rows.
**Shape right sleeve**
Cast off 45 sts at beg of next 2 rows. Work 91 rows. Change to 3mm (US 2) needles and yarn V. P 2 rows to form foldline. Work 16 rows st st, beg with a K row. Cast off.

### NECKBAND
Using double-pointed 3mm (US 2) needles and yarn V, with rs facing K up 140 sts around neck edge. K 1 round. Cast off.

### BACK AND FRONT HEMS (alike)
Using 3mm (US 2) needles and yarn V, with rs facing K up 102 [110,116] sts along lower edge of

*This is such a simple shape, you can easily make it larger or smaller. The colourway shown here is given in the pattern.*

T-shirt. K 2 rows to form hemline. Work 6 rows st st, beg with a P row. Cast off.

## TO MAKE UP
Join side and sleeve seams. Fold cuff edges and hems on to ws and catch down.

## COLOUR SEQUENCE
Work the stripes in the foll sequence; the number refers to the number of rows and the letter refers to the yarn:
5A, 5Q, 1A, 1C, 2Q, 10N, 1S, 1D, 1R, 6M, 3U, 1T, 1F, 1H, 5C, 1U, 2E, 10H, 4R, 1H, 1A, 1D, 2S, 4Q, 1L, 1J, 1C, 2U, 2G, 5T, 3E, 1U, 17[21,25]N, 8M, 3E, 2C, 1A, 1F, 2H, 1M, 1Q, 2T, 1U, 1N, 8Q, 7C, 2J, 1T, 3U, 1A, 1B, 4M, 2D, 1R, 1E, 1N, 2C, 1J, 1F, 2H, 2M, 1D, 3A, 2U, 1J, 1N, 1M, 1T, 1A, 18Q, 2N, 3S, 1D, 6M, 2E, 1T, 1U, 38[42,46]C, 2J, 1M, 7N, 4E, 1T, 1B, 1C, 10T, 3M, 2D, 1R, 1E, 2H, 5B, 3A, 1Q, 1C, 3U, 7N, 2M, 1Q, 2A.

## Striped Skirt

For this I started off thinking of a classic Roman stripe and knitted about twenty swatches in various colour combinations. You will notice that there are strong contrasts as well as several sections where colours 'slide' into each other—magenta into chestnut, royal blue into turquoise, rust into orange, gold into khaki. When colours are close in tone, they can create a harmony that makes the line between them dissolve. After such a section, a stripe in a sharp bright colour followed by a dark one gives this pattern its particular character. I used the more neutral or dark colours for large areas, saving the bright ones for one-row accents (there are 28 colours in all).

You can make the skirt as long or short as you like by working more or fewer rows; if you want it narrower, just cast on fewer stitches.

## MATERIALS
Approx 700g (25oz) mixed yarns and colours averaging double knitting weight
1 each 3mm (US 2), 3¾mm (US 5) and 4½mm (US 7) circular needles
1cm (½in) wide elastic

## TENSION
19 sts and 28 rows to 10cm (4in) over st st on 4½mm (US 7) needles.

## MEASUREMENTS
**To fit hips** up to 111cm (44in)
**Actual width** 174cm (69in)
**Length** 84cm (33in)

## TO MAKE (one piece)
Beg at lower edge, using 3¾mm (US 5) needle and chosen yarn, cast on 330 sts.
Work in st st in rounds, work 13 rounds.
**Next round** P to end to form hemline.
Change to 4½mm (US 7) needle and work 220 rows st st in stripes at random
Change to 3mm (US 2) needle.
**Next round** (K9, K2 tog) to end. 300 sts.
**Next round** (K1, K2 tog) to end. 200 sts.
Work 24 rounds K1, P1 rib. Cast off in rib.

## TO MAKE UP
Fold hem on to ws and catch down. Fold waist ribbing in half on to ws and catch down leaving an opening for elastic.
Cut elastic to waist measurement and insert in waistband. Oversew ends securely. Catch down opening neatly.

## Triangular Shawl

Knitting triangular shawls can be really addictive. They start off easy, and by the time the rows get longer you're really involved. They are also an excellent vehicle for all sorts of improvisations.

For a lightweight summer shawl, try baby wool or four-ply on 3¾mm (US 5) needles—use larger needles if you're carrying lots of colours across the back, or if you knit tightly. A shawl must have drape to it and not be at all stiff or tight. If you want a really quick decorative effect, use chunky yarns and mohair combined on 8mm (US 11) or 9mm (US 13) needles. The main thing to keep in mind is to pick a needle that knits to a nice loose tension with your chosen yarn.

These shawls can be as wide and deep as you please. You just keep increasing at the sides until it's the size you want. This one is only 86cm (34in) deep; the other shawls in this book are about 150cm (5ft) deep and over 250cm (8ft) wide at the top edge. Remember that the fringes, if you have them (and they are half the fun), will add a good deal to the length.

The top edge of the shawl can be finished with a crocheted border, a few rows of garter stitch or a knitted-in hem (work a knit row on the wrong side to form a foldline and work a few rows in stocking stitch, dec 1 st at each end of every row, for the underside). The other two sides usually have fringes. The number of threads per tassel is dictated by the thickness of the yarn—if it's chunky, you might need only two or three strands. I like a good generous length of about 30cm (12in). Sometimes you need a solid colour fringe for simple drama, but often it's better to have rich shades of colour or contrast so that the design is extended in a gorgeous way into the movement of the fringes.

## MATERIALS
Approx 400g (15oz) mixed yarns and colours averaging double knitting weight
1 pair 4½mm (US 7) needles

## TENSION
18 sts and 25 rows to 10cm (4in) over st st on 4½mm (US 7) needles.

## MEASUREMENTS
**Depth** 86cm (34in) including fringe
**Width** 187cm (73½in)

## TO MAKE
Using 4½mm needles (US 7), cast on 3 sts.
K 1 row. Working in st st, in stripes at random, inc 1 st at each end of every row until there are 321 sts. K 8 rows, inc as before. 337 sts. Cast off.

## TO MAKE UP
Make 22cm (8½in) fringe on diagonal edges.

(Overleaf) *Arriving in Holland the day all the tulips were cut, we photographed the striped outfit in the Keukenhof Gardens just outside Amsterdam. This version of the T-shirt is in inky black chenille with pin-stripes of dark colours.* (Inset) *The triangular shawl with luscious black fringes is worn over the striped skirt and the dark Persian Poppy Waistcoat (page 140).*

# Jack's Back Stripe

'Jack's Back' got its name from a waistcoat I knitted for Jack Franses, who once had a famous carpet shop in Piccadilly in London. That waistcoat was one of my first commissions. The fronts had diagonal stripes involving dozens of colours in each row, and we wanted something equally rich-looking but simpler to knit for the back. I had seen some Islamic stonework cut in this pattern and gave it a try.

Although it looks so rich and complex, there are only two colours in each row, so it's quick to knit and a marvellous vehicle for many different schemes. I often use very tweedy merging tones, but quite colourful dramatic contrasts could be exciting. I usually get groups of close colours sorted out so that, for example, a range of browns will follow a range of pinks and then be followed by a range of creams and so on. Of course, you must 'knit in' the yarn not being worked or you will have long loops at the back.

## Blouson Jacket

When I designed the autumn colouring given in the pattern for this jacket, the crimsons, coppers and golds of an English autumn were all around. I used a mixture of chenilles, wool tweeds and plain wools for this one, but I've done many other variations on the jacket and most of them have mohair in them somewhere. It helps lighten the texture. If you want to add some to this jacket, substitute a strand of mohair for one of double knitting where several yarns have been used together (in the first five rows, for example).

A beige colourway was inspired by, of all things, a rain-stained wall in King's Cross in London. Steve suggested I do a colouring restricted to the beiges, soft greys and ivory of a wall we passed one day. The yarns were a luxurious assortment of raw silk, mohair, wool and cotton.

## MATERIALS
**Yarn used**

200g (8oz) Rowan Spun Tweed in tea 752 (A); 75g (3oz) in paprika 754 (B); 50g (2oz) each in tobacco 751 (C), caper 762 (D), cranberry 753 (F) and damson 755 (G); 25g (1oz) in fig 761 (E)

100g (4oz) Rowan Yarns Cotton Chenille in teak 351 (H); 75g (3oz) each in ash beige 353 (J) and french mustard 363 (M); 50g (2oz) in fern 364 (N); 25g (1oz) in lavender 357 (L)

75g (3oz) Rowan Yarns Chunky Tweed in indian red 711 (Q); 50g (2oz) each in crimson pink 701 (R) and blue lovat 705 (S)

125g (5oz) Rowan Yarns Light Tweed in cherrymix 216 (T); 50g (2oz) each in jungle 212 (W) and bracken 204 (Y); 25g (1oz) each in autumn 205 (U), grey 209 (V) and pebble 203 (X)

50g (2oz) Rowan Yarns Double Knitting Wool in brownish red 77 (Z) and red 45 (a)

(Far left) *Jack's Back Blouson in the autumn colouring melting richly into the maples at Westonbirt Arboretum, near Tetbury, Gloucestershire.*

19

## Stripes

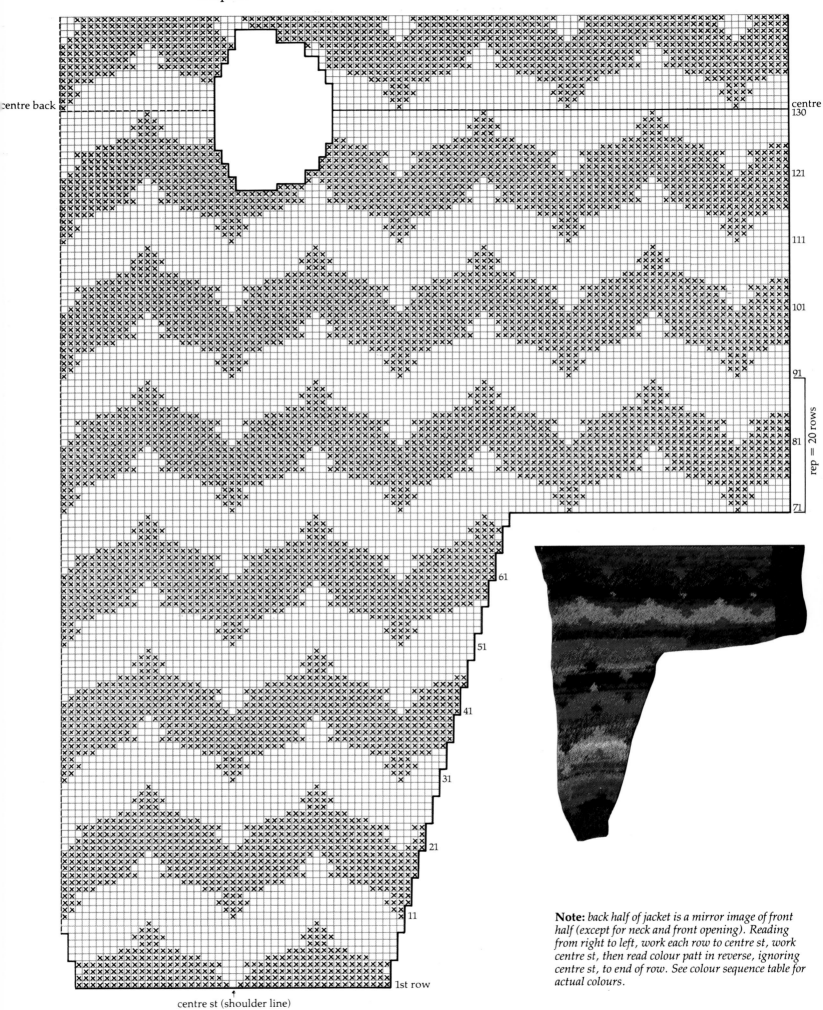

centre back

centre
130

121

111

101

91

rep = 20 rows

81

71

61

51

41

31

21

11

1st row

centre st (shoulder line)

**Note:** *back half of jacket is a mirror image of front half (except for neck and front opening). Reading from right to left, work each row to centre st, work centre st, then read colour patt in reverse, ignoring centre st, to end of row. See colour sequence table for actual colours.*

50g (2oz) Rowan Yarns Fine Cotton Chenille in cardinal 379 (b)
**Equivalent yarn** chunky
1 pair each 5½mm (US 9) and 6½mm (US 10½) needles
6 buttons

NOTE
*The finer yarns are used in combination. For example, 'TUZ' means one strand each of yarns T, U and Z; 'YYY' means three strands of yarn Y. If preferred chunky yarns used singly can be substituted for the combined yarns throughout.*

TENSION
14 sts and 19 rows to 10cm (4in) over patt on 6½mm (US 10½) needles.

MEASUREMENTS
**To fit bust/chest** up to 106cm (42in)
**Actual width** 126cm (49½in)
**Length to shoulder** 64cm (25in)
**Side seam** 36cm (14in)
**Sleeve seam** 43cm (17in)

RIGHT POCKET EDGING
Using 5½mm (US 9) needles and yarns AT, cast on 26 sts.
Work 4 rows K1, P1 rib.
Leave these sts on a spare needle.

LEFT POCKET LINING
Using 6½mm (US 10½) needles and yarns AT, cast on 18 sts.
Work in st st, beg with a K row, inc 1 st at end of 1st and every foll alt row until there are 30 sts, ending with a P row.
**Next row** Cast off 4 sts, K to end.
Leave these sts on a spare needle.

BACK, FRONTS AND SLEEVES (one piece)
Beg at right cuff, using 5½mm (US 9) needles and yarn G, cast on 32 sts.
Change to yarns AT and work 13 rows K1, P1 rib.

## Jack's Back Stripe

*A more subtle colourway with touches of sea green photographed out of season at an English seaside resort.*

**Next row** Rib 4, K up loop between next st and last st to make 1, (rib 2, make 1) to last 4 sts, rib 4. 45 sts.
Change to 6½mm (US 10½) needles and commence colour patt from chart, work in st st throughout, beg with a K row, weaving yarns into back of work, as foll:
**1st row** (rs) K22AU, 1TUZ, 22AU.
**2nd row** P21AU, 3TUZ, 21AU.
Cont in patt as set, changing colours as shown in colour sequence table, *at the same time* inc 1 st at each end of 5th chart row and every foll 4th row until there are 79 sts.
Cont in patt until 70 patt rows have been completed, ending with a P row.

| COLOUR SEQUENCE TABLE | | | | | | | | | | | |
|---|---|---|---|---|---|---|---|---|---|---|---|
| rows | ☒ | ☐ | rows | ☒ | ☐ | rows | ☒ | ☐ | rows | ☒ | ☐ |
| 1–2 | AU | TUZ | 31 | M | NX | 61–64 | H | R | 98–100 | AZ | XYY |
| 3–5 | H | TUZ | 32–33 | M | XXX | 65 | ST | R | 101–102 | H | N |
| 6–7 | H | B | 34–35 | M | J | 66 | A | UUV | 103–106 | H | WWY |
| 8 | G | B | 36–37 | D | J | 67–68 | H | L | 107–110 | H | DW |
| 9–10 | G | CT | 38 | DW | J | 69 | H | Q | 111–115 | B | M |
| 11 | R | TWa | 39 | E | J | 70 | H | ST | 116–117 | TWZ | M |
| 12 | R | B | 40 | NW | J | 71–74 | ba | EY | 118 | TWZ | DD |
| 13–15 | R | TUZ | 41–42 | M | L | 75–77 | ba | S | 119–120 | TWb | DD |
| 16 | R | Q | 43–45 | M | TWZ | 78–79 | TTb | S | 121 | B | G |
| 17–18 | L | Q | 46 | M | Tbb | 80 | R | S | 122 | C | G |
| 19 | S | Q | 47–48 | H | B | 81–84 | GT | C | 123 | C | TTT |
| 20 | A | bb | 49–50 | H | BY | 85–86 | FT | C | 124–126 | BU | TTT |
| 21 | R | J | 51–52 | G | BY | 87 | FT | CY | 127 | BU | R |
| 22–24 | CT | J | 53 | AT | BY | 88 | FT | YYY | 128 | bb | L |
| 25 | L | J | 54–55 | AT | Q | 89 | bb | YYY | 129 | bb | FV |
| 26 | CV | J | 56 | FZ | Q | 90 | bb | JY | 130 | bb | GT |
| 27 | CV | UXY | 57 | H | YYY | 91–93 | Q | JY | | | |
| 28–29 | R | UXY | 58–59 | FG | YYY | 94–96 | Q | JX | | | |
| 30 | R | J | 60 | H | YYY | 97 | Q | XYY | | | |

Stripes

**Shape front and back**
**Next row** With yarn A, cast on 40 sts, work 71st patt row across all 119 sts.
Using yarn A, cast on 40 sts on to free needle and cont 71st row across these sts for back. 159 sts.
Cont in patt without shaping until 80th patt row has been completed.
**Place right pocket**
**81st row** Patt 6 sts, sl next 26 sts on a length of yarn for pocket lining, now to join in right pocket edging, patt across 26 sts left on first spare needle, then patt to end of row.
Cont in patt until 118th patt row has been completed.
**Divide for neck**
**Next row** Patt 73 sts, turn, leaving rem sts on a spare needle for back, cont on these sts only for right front.
**Shape front neck**
Cont in patt, cast off 4 sts at beg of next row, then 2 sts at beg of foll alt row. Now dec 1 st at beg of foll 2 alt rows. 65 sts.
Work straight until 130th patt row has been completed. Using yarns GT, cast off.
**Shape back neck**
With rs facing, rejoin yarn to sts left on spare needle for back.
Cast off 6 sts, patt to end. Work 1 row.
Dec 1 st at beg of next and foll 2 alt rows. 77 sts.
Work straight for 10 rows, keeping patt correct but reversing colour sequence table after 130th row by working colours for 130th row again, then those for 129th row, 128th row, 127th row, 126th row and so on.
Now inc 1 st at end of next and foll 2 alt rows.
Work 2 rows straight, turn and cast on 6 sts at end of last row. 86 sts.
Leave these sts.
**Work left front**
Using 6½mm (US 10½) needles and yarns GT, cast on 65 sts.
Commence colour patt from chart, work in st st, beg with a K row, work 5 rows straight reversing colour sequence table, beg with 130th row.
**Shape front neck**
Inc 1 st at beg of next and foll alt row.
Work 1 row, then cast on 2 sts at beg of next row and 4 sts at beg of foll alt row. 73 sts.
**Join back and front**
Work next row across these 73 sts, then across 86 sts left for back. 159 sts.
Cont in patt without shaping, keeping patt layout correct but working backwards through colour sequence table as before until 50 patt rows have been completed, ending with a P row.
**Place left pocket**
**Next row** Patt 6 sts, sl next 26 sts on a length of yarn for left pocket edging, patt across left pocket lining sts on second spare needle, patt to end.
Cont in patt, work 7 rows.
**Shape left sleeve**
**Next row** Using yarn A, K40 sts, patt 79 sts, K40A.
**Next row** With A, cast off 40 sts, patt 79 sts, cast off 40 sts in A. 79 sts.
Work 1 row.
Now dec 1 st at each end of next and every foll 4th row until 45 sts rem.
Work 4 rows straight.

**Shape cuff**
Change to 5½mm (US 9) needles and yarns AT, and work in K1, P1 rib as foll:
**Next row** K1, P1, (K1, P2 tog) to last 4 sts, (K1, P1) twice. 32 sts.
Rib 13 rows.
Cast off in rib in G.

RIGHT POCKET LINING
With rs facing sl 26 sts left at right pocket opening on to 6½mm (US 10½) needles.
Using yarns AT, K 1 row.
Cont in st st, dec 1 st at beg of next row, cast on 4 sts at beg of foll alt row, then dec 1 st at beg of next and every foll alt row until 18 sts rem.
Cast off.

LEFT POCKET EDGING
With rs facing sl 26 sts left at left pocket opening on to 5½mm (US 9) needles. Using yarns AT, work 4 rows K1, P1 rib.
Cast off in rib.

TO MAKE UP
Catch down pocket edges.
Catch down pocket linings to ws of fronts.
Backstitch side and sleeve seams.
**Welt**
Using 5½mm (US 9) needles and yarns AT, with rs facing, K up 182 sts around bottom edge of jacket.
Work 12 rows K1, P1 rib.
Cast off in rib loosely in G.
**Button band**
Using 5½mm (US 9) needles and yarns AT, with rs facing, K up 77 sts (65 sts on main part and 12 sts on welt) along right front edge (for man's jacket, left front edge for woman's).
P 1 row, then K 2 rows to form foldline. Using yarn A only, work 8 rows st st, beg with a K row.
Cast off loosely.
**Buttonhole band**
Using 5½mm (US 9) needles and yarns AT, with rs of work facing, K up 77 sts as for button band (along left front edge for man's jacket, right front edge for woman's), *at the same time* make buttonholes on K up row as foll:
**K up and buttonhole row** K up 2 sts, (K up 2 sts, lift 2nd st on right-hand needle over 1st st and off needle, K up 1 st, lift 2nd st on right-hand needle over 1st st and off needle, K up 11 sts) 6 times, ending last rep K up 2.
**Next row** P to end, casting on 2 sts over those cast off in previous row. 77 sts.
K 2 rows to form foldline.
**Next row** Using yarn A only, K2, (cast off 2 sts, K12 including st used to cast off) to last 5 sts, cast off 2 sts, K to end.
**Next row** P to end, casting on 2 sts over those cast off in previous row.
Work 6 rows st st, beg with a K row.
Cast off loosely.
Fold button and buttonhole bands on to ws and catch down.
**Collar**
Using 5½mm (US 9) needles and yarns AT, with rs facing, K up 72 sts evenly round neck edge.
Work 12 rows K1, P1 rib. Cast off in rib in G.
Neaten buttonholes. Sew on buttons.

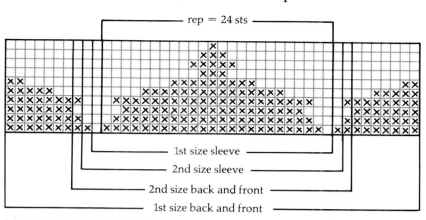

## Jack's Back Stripe

rep = 24 sts

1st size sleeve
2nd size sleeve
2nd size back and front
1st size back and front

# V-neck Sweater

Living in Britain since 1964 has made me come to terms with grey. Ever since I used it in some of my early waistcoats and striped pullovers, grey has had a mysterious bearing for me, that I return to over and over again with great relish. It is a colour that is really flattering to the delicate colouring of Western skin and eye tones, and the tweedy yarns work excellently here to give atmosphere to a classic V-necked sweater.

## MATERIALS
**Yarn used**
100g (4oz) Rowan Yarns Double Knitting Wool in pale grey 59 (C); 75g (3oz) in charcoal 61 (B); 25[50]g (1[2]oz) in blue/grey 88 (A); 25g (1oz) in fawn 82 (D)
50[75]g (2[3]oz) Rowan Yarns Cotton Chenille in driftwood 352 (E)
50[75]g (2[3]oz) Rowan Yarns Fine Cotton Chenille in shark 378 (F)
100[125]g (4[5]oz) Rowan Spun Tweed in caviar 760 (L); 100g (4oz) in fig 761 (H); 50g (2oz) each in caper 762 (G) and damson 755 (J)
100[125]g (4[5]oz) Rowan Yarns Light Tweed in grey 209 (N); 50g (2oz) each in atlantic 223 (M), charcoal 210 (Q), autumn 205 (R) and champagne 202 (T); 25g (1oz) each in lavender 213 (S) and silver 208 (U)
**Equivalent yarn** Aran/medium-weight
1 pair each 4mm (US 6) and 5mm (US 8) needles

## NOTE
*The finer yarns are used in combination. For example, 'MN' means one strand each of yarns M and N; 'BB' means two strands of B. If preferred Aran-weight yarns used singly can be substituted for the combined yarns.*

## TENSION
19 sts and 22 rows to 10cm (4in) over patt on 5mm (US 8) needles.

## MEASUREMENTS
**To fit bust/chest** 86–91[96–101]cm (34–36[38–40]in)
**Actual width** 96[106]cm (38[42]in)
**Length to shoulder** 65[68]cm (25½[26½]in)
**Side seam** 41cm (16in)
**Sleeve seam** 46[48]cm (18[19]in)

## BACK
Using 4mm (US 6) needles and yarn L, cast on 81[89] sts. Work in K1, P1 rib as foll: (2 rows in L, 2 rows in H) 4 times, 1 row in L.
**Next row** With L (work into front and back of next st to inc 1, rib 7) to last st, rib 1 [inc 1]. 91[101] sts.
Change to 5mm (US 8) needles and commence colour patt from chart (above), working in st st throughout and weaving contrast colours into back of work, as foll:
**1st row** (rs) K 9 [2]G, (1AM, 23G) 3[4] times, 1AM, 9 [2]G.
**2nd row** P8 [1]G, 2AM, (1AM, 21G, 2AM) 3[4] times, 1AM, 8 [1]G.
Cont in patt as set foll colour sequence table for colour changes, rep 1st–10th rows until 78 patt rows have been worked, ending with a ws row.

## COLOUR SEQUENCE TABLE

| rows | ☒ | ☐ | rows | ☒ | ☐ |
|---|---|---|---|---|---|
| 1–2 | G | AM | 71 | E | H |
| 3–4 | E | AM | 72–73 | BQ | H |
| 5–6 | H | AM | 74 | L | H |
| 7–10 | BB | MN | 75–77 | J | H |
| 11–12 | FM | J | 78–80 | J | RN |
| 13 | FM | QQ | 81 | RN | MC |
| 14 | FN | QQ | 82 | H | MC |
| 15–18 | CN | QB | 83–84 | RR | MC |
| 19–20 | CN | NB | 85–86 | RN | MC |
| 21–22 | BN | H | 87–89 | RN | CU |
| 23 | DQ | H | 90 | RN | CT |
| 24–27 | NN | H | 91–93 | CT | BQ |
| 28–29 | NN | RS | 94–95 | NT | BQ |
| 30 | NN | G | 96 | NN | BQ |
| 31–33 | RR | FT | 97–99 | NN | BM |
| 34 | RN | FT | 100 | NN | E |
| 35–37 | RN | CU | 101–102 | BS | J |
| 38–39 | RN | TU | 103 | BQ | J |
| 40 | RN | FC | 104 | E | J |
| 41 | FC | E | 105 | BQ | J |
| 42–44 | TC | E | 106–110 | BN | L |
| 45–47 | TT | QA | 111 | J | G |
| 48 | TT | MF | 112 | AQ | G |
| 49 | TT | E | 113–116 | L | G |
| 50 | TT | CN | 117–119 | AQ | G |
| 51–53 | MF | CC | 120 | AQ | H |
| 54–58 | NF | CC | 121–123 | H | NN |
| 59–60 | NM | NC | 124–125 | E | NN |
| 61 | NC | L | 126–130 | G | NN |
| 62–65 | FN | L | 131–134 | NU | EE |
| 66–68 | FS | L | 135–137 | UU | BF |
| 69–70 | MS | L | 138–140 | TU | BF |

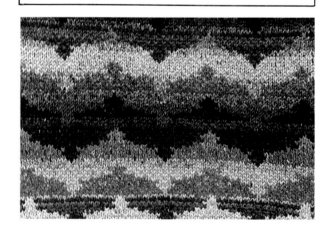

*This close-up of the Jack's Back Sweater fabric with its subtle tweedy tones suggests to me mountain ranges veiled in mist.*

Stripes

**Shape armholes**
Cast off 10 sts at beg of next 2 rows. 71[81] sts.**
Now work straight until 130[134] patt rows in all
have been worked, ending with a ws row.
**Shape shoulders and divide for back neck**
**Next row** Cast off 6[8] sts, patt 21[24] sts, turn,
leaving rem sts on a spare needle and cont on
these sts only for right side of neck.
Cast off 5 sts at beg of next row, 6[8] sts at beg of
foll row and 4 sts at beg of foll alt row.
Cast off rem 6[7] sts.
With rs facing rejoin yarn to neck edge, cast off 17
sts, patt to end. 27[32] sts.
**Next row** Cast off 6[8] sts, patt to end.
Complete left side to match right.

FRONT
Work as given for back to **.
**Divide for neck**
**Next row** Patt 33[38] sts, K2 tog, turn, leaving
rem sts on a spare needle and cont on these sts
only for left side of neck. 34[39] sts.
Dec 1 st at neck edge on every foll 3rd row until
18[23] sts rem.
Now work straight until front matches back to
shoulder, ending at armhole edge.
**Shape shoulder**
Cast off 6[8] sts at beg of next and foll alt row.
Work 1 row. Cast off.
Return to sts on spare needle, sl centre st on to
safety pin. With rs facing rejoin yarn to next st,
K2 tog, patt to end.
Complete right side to match left.

SLEEVES
Using 4mm (US 6) needles and yarn L, cast on
41[43] sts.
Work 17 rows K1, P1 rib as given for back.
**Next row** Rib 1[3], (inc 1, rib 5) to end. 49[51] sts.
Change to 5mm (US 8) needles and commence
colour patt from chart working between sleeve
markers, *at the same time* inc 1 st at each end of
every foll 4th row until there are 89 [99] sts.
Now work straight until 100[104] patt rows have
been completed.
Cast off.

TO MAKE UP
Backstitch right shoulder seam.
**Neckband**
Using 4mm (US 6) needles and yarn L, with rs
facing K up 50[56] sts down left side of neck, K
centre st from safety pin, K up 50[56] sts up right
side of neck and 42 sts across back neck. 143[155]
sts. Work in K1, P1 rib as foll:
**Next row** With L, rib to within 2 sts of centre st,
P2 tog, P1, P2 tog tbl, rib to end. 141[153] sts.
**Next row** With H, rib to within 2 sts of centre st,
K2 tog tbl, K1, K2 tog, rib to end. 139[151] sts.
Cont to dec in this way on each side of centre st,
working knitwise decs on rs rows and purlwise
decs on ws rows, as foll: 1 row in H, 2 rows in L, 2
rows in H, 1 row in L.
Cast off in rib in L.
Backstitch left shoulder seam.
Set in sleeves matching centre of cast-off edge to
shoulder seam and joining last few rows of sleeve
to cast-off sts at underarm.
Join side and sleeve seams.

*(Far right)* Jack's Back
V-neck Sweater in my
studio specially painted by
Robert Buys. We painted
and repainted this room
with many different
backdrops for our colour
schemes. See the other sets
on pages 26, 48, 97, 53,
108, 113, 116, 119, 125
and 152.

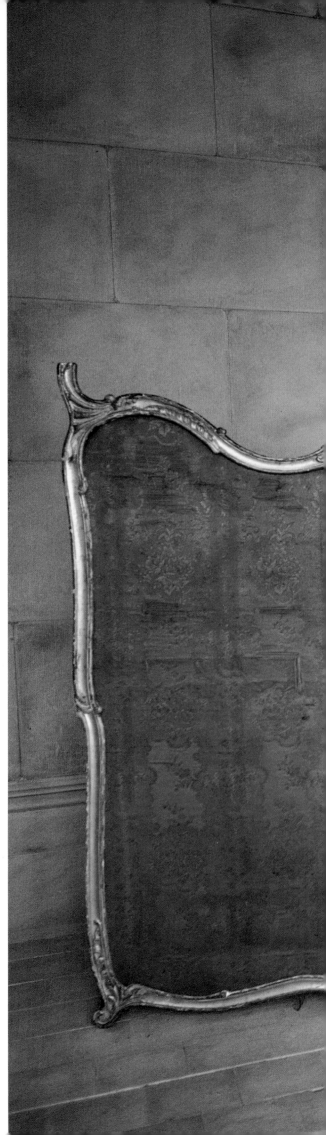

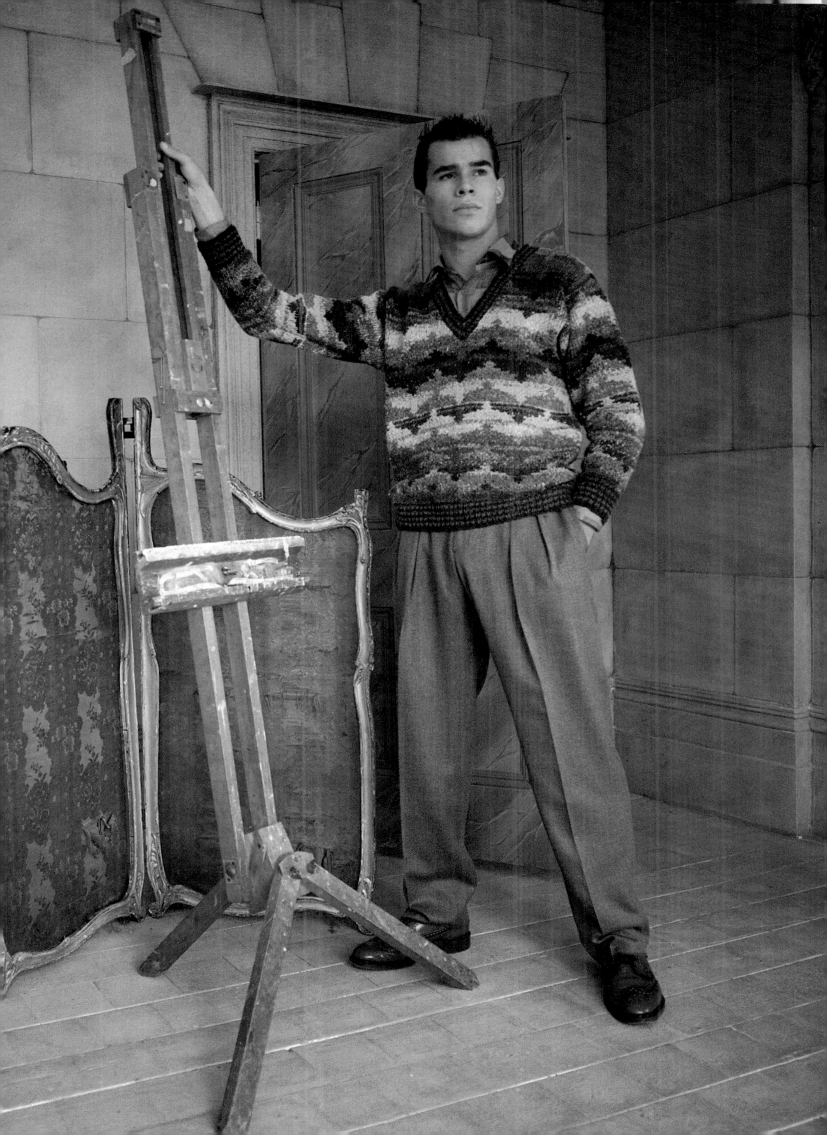

Stripes

# Peplum Jacket

Brown marble streaked with rich veins of maroon and moss greens on deep beige and grey grounds was the inspiration for the colouring of this tight-fitting jacket. I was also thinking of certain tweedy ladies who look wonderful in grey pearls and smoky grey-browns. It can be worn on its own with a tweed skirt or, perhaps, with a warm grey silk blouse.

## MATERIALS
**Yarn used**
100g (4oz) Rowan Yarns Double Knitting Wool in charcoal 61 (F); 75g (3oz) in blue/grey 88 (G); 50g (2oz) each in dark brown 80 (A), dark brownish red 71 (C), mid grey 129 (D) and coffee 616 (E); 25g (1oz) each in dark green/brown 407 (B) and fawn 82 (H)
75g (3oz) Rowan Yarns Fine Cotton Chenille in mole 380 (L); 50g (2oz) in shark 378 (M); 25g (1oz) each in plum 386 (J), lacquer 388 (N) and purple 384 (Q)
50g (2oz) Rowan Yarns Light Tweed each in autumn 205 (R) and grey 209 (T); 25g (1oz) each in jungle 212 (S), lakeland 222 (U), charcoal 210 (V), lavender 213 (W) and atlantic 223 (X)
**Equivalent yarn** double knitting
1 pair each 3¼mm (US 3) and 4mm (US 6) needles
5 buttons

## TENSION
22 sts and 26 rows to 10cm (4in) over patt on 4mm (US 6) needles.

## MEASUREMENTS
**To fit bust** 81–86[86–91]cm (32–34[34–36]in)
**Actual underarm width** 91[96]cm (36[38]in)
**Length to shoulder** 53cm (21in) including peplum
**Side seam** 24cm (9½in) excluding peplum
**Sleeve seam** 45cm (17½in)

## BACK
Using 4mm (US 6) needles and yarn A, cast on 85[89] sts.
Work in st st beg with a K row, commence colour patt from chart 1 (page 28), weaving contrast colours into back of work, as foll:
**1st row** (rs) K0[2]A, *18A, 1B, 5A; rep from * to last 13[15] sts, 13[15]A.
**2nd row** P13[15]A, *4A, 3B, 17A; rep from * to last 0[2] sts, 0[2]A.
Cont in patt as set foll colour sequence table for colour changes, rep 1st–20th rows, *at the same time* inc 1 st at each end of 7th and every foll 6th row until there are 101[105] sts.
Work straight until 62 patt rows have been completed.
**Shape armholes**
Keeping patt correct, cast off 5 sts at beg of next 2 rows, then dec 1 st at each end of foll 5 alt rows. 81[85] sts. Now work straight until 110 patt rows have been completed.
**Shape shoulders and divide for back neck**
**Next row** Cast off 8[10] sts, patt 25 sts including st used to cast off, cast off 15 sts, patt to end.
**Next row** Cast off 8[10] sts, patt to neck edge, turn, leaving rem sts on a spare needle and cont on these sts only for left side of neck. 25 sts.

*(Far right) This is the colourway specified in the pattern. I particularly like the way the warm shades of the jacket tone with the bloom on the plums.*

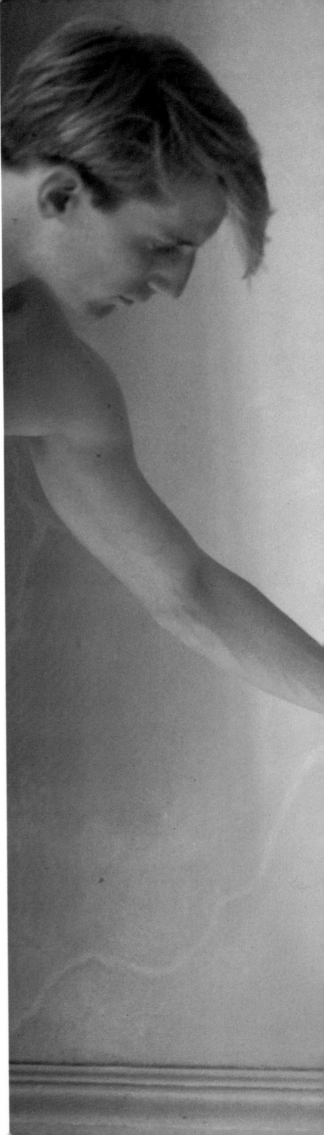

## Stripes

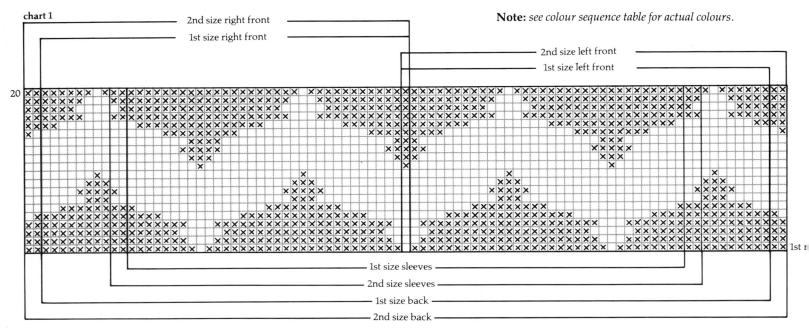

chart 1

2nd size right front

1st size right front

**Note:** *see colour sequence table for actual colours.*

2nd size left front

1st size left front

20

1st r

1st size sleeves

2nd size sleeves

1st size back

2nd size back

| COLOUR SEQUENCE TABLE | | | | | |
|---|---|---|---|---|---|
| **rows** | ⊠ | ☐ | **rows** | ⊠ | ☐ |
| 1–2 | A | B | 63 | T | W |
| 3–4 | C | D | 64 | M | G |
| 5–6 | C | R | 65 | D | G |
| 7–9 | J | E | 66 | D | F |
| 10–11 | J | R | 67–70 | D | G |
| 12–13 | J | L | 71 | E | R |
| 14–15 | F | L | 72 | E | F |
| 16 | A | L | 73 | E | G |
| 17 | S | L | 74 | E | W |
| 18 | C | L | 75 | E | F |
| 19 | F | L | 76–79 | L | F |
| 20 | S | L | 80 | R | F |
| 21–22 | S | G | 81 | R | H |
| 23–24 | B | T | 82 | L | H |
| 25 | B | G | 83 | V | H |
| 26 | B | M | 84–85 | S | H |
| 27–28 | B | T | 86 | R | M |
| 29 | B | U | 87 | L | M |
| 30 | B | M | 88 | L | T |
| 31 | H | M | 89 | L | H |
| 32–34 | H | U | 90 | L | D |
| 35 | E | U | 91–92 | N | D |
| 36–37 | E | M | 93 | N | M |
| 38 | H | M | 94 | N | L |
| 39–40 | R | M | 95 | F | L |
| 41–42 | R | C | 96–98 | C | R |
| 43–44 | L | C | 99–100 | F | R |
| 45–46 | E | C | 101 | T | G |
| 47 | E | N | 102 | L | G |
| 48 | E | F | 103–104 | F | G |
| 49 | E | S | 105 | N | G |
| 50 | E | C | 106 | N | X |
| 51–52 | M | A | 107 | J | X |
| 53–54 | G | A | 108–109 | J | U |
| 55 | G | Q | 110 | J | M |
| 56 | T | C | 111–112 | F | U |
| 57–58 | M | C | 113 | F | W |
| 59–60 | M | A | 114–115 | F | G |
| 61–62 | D | W | 116 | F | |

Cast off 5 sts at beg of next row, 8 sts at beg of foll row and 5 sts at beg of foll row.
Cast off rem 7 sts.
Rejoin yarn to sts on spare needle and complete right side of neck to match left side.

**LEFT FRONT**
Using 4mm (US 6) needles and yarn A, cast on 43[45] sts.
Work in st st, beg with a K row, commence colour patt from chart 1 working between left front markers, *at the same time* inc 1 st at beg of 7th and every foll 6th row until there are 51[53] sts.
Now work straight until 62 patt rows have been completed, ending with a P row.
**Shape armhole**
Cast off 5 sts at beg of next row, then dec 1 st at armhole edge on foll 5 alt rows. 41[43] sts.
Now work straight until 93 patt rows have been completed, ending with a K row.
**Shape neck**
Cast off 5 sts at beg of next row, then 3 sts at beg of foll alt row. Now dec 1 st at neck edge on next 6 rows and on foll 4 alt rows. 23[25] sts (110 patt rows have been completed, ending at armhole edge).
**Shape shoulder**
Cast off 8[10] sts at beg of next row and 8 sts at beg of foll alt row. Work 1 row. Cast off.

**RIGHT FRONT**
Work as given for left front reversing all shapings and foll chart between right front markers.

**SLEEVES**
Using 3¼mm (US 3) needles and yarn A, cast on 47[51] sts.
Work 22 rows K1, P1 rib as foll: 3 rows in A, 3 rows in C, 2 rows in V, 1 row in B, A, V, G, A, R, 2 rows in G, 2 rows in R, 3 rows in F, 1 row in S.
Cont in rib for 52 rows, inc 1 st at each end of next and every foll 6th row as foll: 1 row in D, V, G, 4 rows in D, 1 row in G, V, D, 3 rows in E, 1 row in G, U, E, H, F, D, 2 rows in H, 1 row in D, X, B, C, 4 rows in E, 1 row in F, 2 rows in R, 1 row in L, 2 rows in G, 1 row in H, 2 rows in L, 4 rows in E, 1

row in R, F, 2 rows in U, 3 rows in D, 3 rows in F. 65[69] sts.

Change to 4mm (US 6) needles and, working in st st beg with a K row, commence colour patt from chart 1 working between sleeve markers, *at the same time* inc 1 st at each end of 5th and every foll 4th row until there are 85[93] sts, and then on every alt row until there are 105 sts.

Now work straight until 62 patt rows have been completed, ending with a P row.

**Shape top**

Cast off 5 sts at beg of next 2 rows, then dec 1 st at each end of next and every foll alt row until 89 sts rem. Work 1 row. Now dec 1 st at each end of next and every foll 4th row until there are 71 sts. Work 3 rows. Dec 1 st at each end of next and every alt row until 59 sts rem.

**Next row** P1, (P2 tog) to end. Cast off.

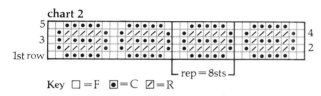

**chart 2**

Key □ =F ☉ =C ☑ =R

## BUTTON BAND

Using 4mm (US 6) needles and yarn F, with rs facing K up 73 sts along left front edge.

**1st–5th rows** Work in st st, foll colour patt from chart 2, beg with a P row.

**6th–8th rows** K 3 rows in F, to form foldline.

**9th–15th rows** Work in st st in A, beg with a P row. Cast off.

## BUTTONHOLE BAND

Work as given for left front band but make buttonholes on 3rd and 11th rows as foll:

**Buttonhole row** Patt 4 sts, (yrn, P2 tog, patt 14 sts) 4 times, yrn, P2 tog, patt to end.

## TO MAKE UP

Backstitch shoulder seams.

**Neck edging**

Using 3¼mm (US 3) needles and yarn F, with rs facing K up 106 sts evenly around neck edge. K 1 row. Cast off.

Join side seams.

**Peplum**

Using 4mm (US 6) needles and yarn A, with rs facing K up 167 [177] sts around lower edge of jacket. Work in st st, beg with a P row.

**1st row** (ws) P6A, (5F, 5A) to last st, 1A.

**2nd row** K6A, (5F, 5A) to last st, 1A.

**3rd row** As 1st row.

**4th row** As 2nd row using C instead of A.

**5th row** P6B, (5D, 5B) to last st, 1B.

**6th row** K6S, (2D, K up loop between next st and last st to make 1, 3D, 2S, make 1, 3S) to last 11 sts, 2D, make 1, 3D, 6S. 198[210] sts.

Cont in this way working in st st panels as set, *at the same time* make 1 st in centre of every panel except the end ones, as in 6th row, on 4 foll 4th rows and using yarns in foll sequence: 1 row S and D, 2 rows R and T, 1 row F and T, 2 rows L and T, 2 rows E and U, 1 row E and H, 1 row E and T, 1 row L and T, 1 row G and H, 2 rows G and T, 1 row F and T, 1 row L and T, 2 rows G and T, 5 rows L and T. 322[342] sts.

Change to 3¼mm (US 3) needles and yarn F. K 3 rows for foldline.

Work in st st beg with a P row, dec 1 st at each end of next 3 rows. Cast off.

**Peplum edging**

Using 3¼mm (US 3) needles and yarn F, with rs facing K up 28 sts down left front of peplum. K 2 rows to form foldline. Work 3 rows st st beg with a P row, dec 1 st at beg of 1st row, 1 st at end of 2nd row and 1 st at beg of 3rd row. Cast off. Work right front edging as for left, reversing shaping.

Join sleeve seams. Set in sleeves making three pleats each side of shoulder seam, matching patt across body and sleeve tops.

Fold hem and edgings on to ws and catch down. Neaten buttonholes. Sew on buttons.

*Dove grey chenille was a wonderful ground for these rainbow pastels. This complete contrast to the other scheme shows how you can take a design like this in many different directions.*

# Ikat Stripe

True *ikat* is the pattern which results from weaving warp threads dyed in two or more colours. To suggest the 'accidents' that are the result of this process, I use two colours which meet at different places, apparently at random. The secret is to jog backwards and forwards with the two colours, never hitting the same place twice. It's a great pattern to knit, as the complex bits are punctuated by restful one-colour sections.

## Batwing Sweater

The sweater (see page 32) is knitted all in one piece from cuff to cuff. The black colourway uses black chenille and some lurex in deep rich tones to go with lighter brightly coloured wools. The dusky lacquer sweater (for which the colours are specified in the pattern) is almost all chenille, with wool in the hems and neck for elasticity.

*Ikat is an oriental weaving technique and you can see it here in the boldest colours in a length of Indian cotton.*

### MATERIALS
**Yarn used**
200g (8oz) Rowan Yarns Fine Cotton Chenille in lacquer 388 (C); 50g (2oz) each in plum 386 (B),

black 377 (D), steel 382 (E), mole 380 (F), purple 384 (G) and cyclamen 385 (L); 25g (1oz) each in turquoise 383 (A), cardinal 379 (H), shark 378 (J) and saville 387 (M)
25g (1oz) Rowan Yarns Double Knitting Wool in black 62 (N)
75g (3oz) Rowan Yarns Light Tweed in cherrymix 215 (Q)
**Equivalent yarn** double knitting
1 pair each 3¼mm (US 3) and 4mm (US 6) needles
1 set each four double-pointed 3¼mm (US 3) and 4mm (US 6) needles (or circular needles)

### TENSION
22 sts and 28 rows to 10cm (4in) over patt on 4mm (US 6) needles.

### MEASUREMENTS
**To fit bust** up to 91cm (36in)
**Length to shoulder** 54cm (21½in)

### BACK, FRONT AND SLEEVES (one piece)
Beg at left cuff, using 3¼mm (US 3) needles and yarn N, cast on 49 sts. Work 6 rows st st, beg with a K row. K 2 rows to form hemline.
Change to 4mm (US 6) needles and cont in st st, twisting yarns between colours to avoid holes, as foll:
**\*\*1st row** (rs) K7A, 7B, 7C, 7D, 7E, 7F, 7B.
**2nd row** P7B, 7F, 7E, 7D, 7C, 7B, 7A.
**3rd–20th rows** Rep 1st–2nd rows 9 times more.
**21st row** K7G, 7H, 7J, 7G, 7D, 7L, 7F.
**22nd row** P7F, 7L, 7D, 7G, 7J, 7H, 7G.
**23rd–30th rows** Rep 21st–22nd rows 4 times more.\*
Cont in st st, work 31st–40th rows in colour patt from chart 1, *at the same time* inc 1 st at each end of next and every alt row. 59 sts.
Cont in st st, beg with a K row, inc 1 st at each end of next and every alt row until there are 157 sts, then inc 1 st at each end of every row until there are 171 sts, *at the same time* commence ikat patt as foll:
**1st–13th rows** Work 6 rows in C, 1 row in G, 6 rows in C.
**14th–19th rows** Work colour patt from chart 2 working inc sts into patt and foll colour sequence table for actual colours.
**20th–32nd rows** As 1st–13th rows using D instead of G.
**33rd–42nd rows** Work colour patt from chart 3, working inc sts into patt and foll colour sequence table for actual colours.
These 42 rows form the ikat patt rep.
Rep 1st–42nd rows using L instead of G on 7th row and H instead of D on 26th row, and foll chart 4 instead of chart 2 on 14th–19th rows.
Now rep 1st–22nd rows using E instead of G and foll chart 5 instead of chart 2.
**Shape back and front**
Cont in patt as set, cast on 33 sts at beg of next 2 rows. 237 sts. Now work 25th–42nd patt rows using J instead of D.
Rep 1st–7th rows using A instead of G, thus ending with a rs row.

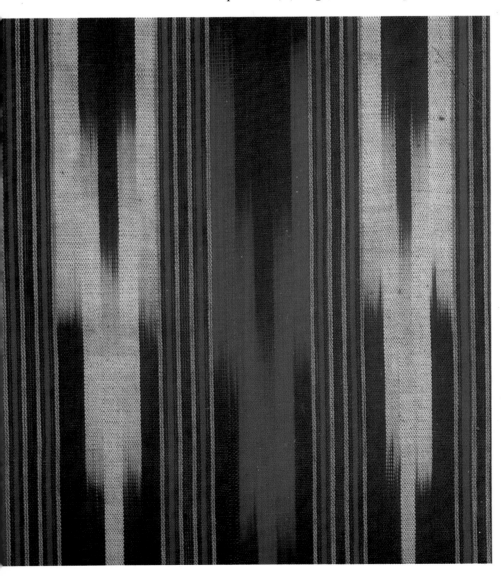

## Divide for neck

**Next row** P114C, cast off 9 sts, P to end in C.
**Next row** K112C, K2C tog, turn, leaving rem sts on a spare needle and cont on these sts only for front. 113 sts.
Cont in patt, work 10th–36th rows foll chart 6 instead of chart 2 and using G instead of D, *at the same time* dec 1 st at neck edge on next 8 rows, then dec 1 st at the neck edge on the foll 3 alt rows. 102 sts.
Cont in patt, work 1 row (37th patt row—this point marks the centre front).
Work 38th–42nd patt rows to complete centre stripe. Cont in patt reversing colour and chart sequence from centre, work 1st–10th rows without shaping.
Now work 11th–25th rows foll chart 6 instead of chart 2, *at the same time* inc 1 st at neck edge on next and 3 foll alt rows, then inc 1 st at neck edge on foll 8 rows. 114 sts.
Leave these sts on a spare needle; with rs facing rejoin yarn to sts on first spare needle.
Work back foll charts and using colours as for front but dec for back neck as foll:
Dec 1 st at neck edge on foll 3 alt rows. Work 47 rows straight, now inc 1 st at neck edge on next and foll 2 alt rows, ending with a rs row.
**Next row** Patt to end, turn and cast on 9 sts, turn and patt across the sts for front left on a spare needle. 237 sts.
Cont in patt across all 237 sts, work right side to match left reversing colour and chart sequence from centre and all shapings, ending with 32nd patt row at right cuff. 59 sts.
Now work cuff patt from chart 1, reading chart from top to bottom, work 40th–31st rows dec 1 st at each end of 1st and every foll alt row. 49 sts.
Now cont in st st, reverse cuff patt as given for left sleeve, working from * to **.
Change to 3¼mm (US 3) needles and yarn N.
K 2 rows to form hemline.
Work 6 rows st st, beg with a K row.
Cast off.

## HEM

Using 3¼mm (US 3) needles and yarn N, with rs facing K up 90 sts along lower front edge.
P 2 rows to form foldline. Work 7 rows st st, beg with a P row.
Cast off loosely.
Work back hem to match.

## COLLAR

Using double-pointed 3¼mm (US 3) needles and yarn Q, with rs facing K up 136 sts evenly around neck edge.
Work 9cm (3½in) K1, P1 rib.
Change to double-pointed 4mm (US 6) needles and Q double.
Cont in K1, P1 rib as foll: 6 rounds in Q double, 1 round in E, 6 rounds in Q double, 1 round in A, 6 rounds in Q double, 1 round in L, 6 rounds in Q double, 1 round in H, 6 rounds in Q double.
Cast off in rib in yarn D.

## TO MAKE UP

Join side and sleeve seams.
Fold hems at cuffs and waist on to ws of work and catch down.

## Ikat Stripe

**Chart 1**

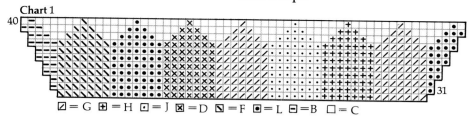

☑ = G  ⊞ = H  ⊡ = J  ⊠ = D  ◨ = F  ⊡ = L  ⊟ = B  ☐ = C

**Chart 2**

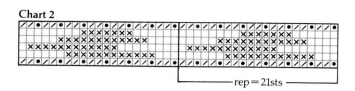

rep = 21sts

**Chart 3**

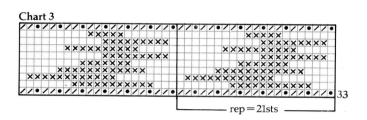

rep = 21sts

**Chart 4**

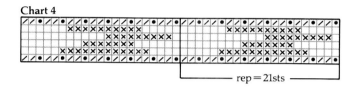

rep = 21sts

**Chart 5**

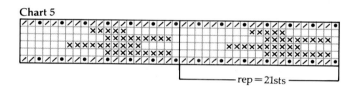

rep = 21sts

**Chart 6**

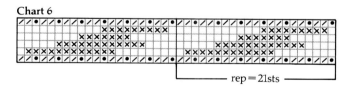

rep = 21sts

**Note:** *see colour sequence table for actual colours.*

| COLOUR SEQUENCE TABLE | ⊡ | ☑ | ☐ | ⊠ |
|---|---|---|---|---|
| chart 2 | A | H | B | L |
| chart 3: | | | | |
| 1st rep | J | B | F | G |
| 2nd rep | H | E | J | L |
| 3rd rep | H | F | D | G |
| 4th rep | L | J | B | H |
| chart 4 | A | G | E | B |
| chart 5 | L | B | F | A |
| chart 6 | B | H | E | L |

*(Overleaf) The red version of the Ikat Striped Batwing photographed on the Alexandre III bridge in Paris. (Inset) The black colourway in the grassy meadows of Hampstead Heath in London.*

# Toothed Stripe

This sprightly pattern came from a Mediterranean embroidery that I saw years ago and couldn't get out of my head. It's less intensive than some of my all-over patterns. There are plain rows, then rows which are alternating bars of colour, then the tricky bits with the 'teeth', and then the peaceful quick plain rows of background colour again. For some reason I always visualize this in lively colours, though it could certainly be done in subtle ones—greys, pale browns and so on.

   The main thing is to make each section of 'teeth' slightly different. You can start each tooth off with three stitches, then on the next row make it three or two, and on the next row two or one in one direction or the other. If you feel more at ease working from a chart, plan out your variations on graph paper. I prefer to improvise on the spot by not repeating what I've already done. The chart gives you the first two pattern repeats to get you going. If in doubt, try the waistcoat on page 37 before launching into the sweater.

## V-neck Sweater

MATERIALS
Approx 750g (27oz) mixed yarns and colours averaging double knitting weight
1 pair each 3¾mm (US 5) and 4½mm (US 7) needles

TENSION
19 sts and 26 rows to 10cm (4in) over patt on 4½mm (US 7) needles.

(Far right) *The Toothed Stripe Sweater was commissioned by a man who wanted flaming red extrovert colours. The turquoises and magentas really spark the reds and its large drapy shape looks delicious on slim figures too. Photographed here with the Persian Poppy Waistcoat (page 140) and below with the Large Diamond Jacket (page 68) on the same day in Regent's Park in London.*

## Stripes

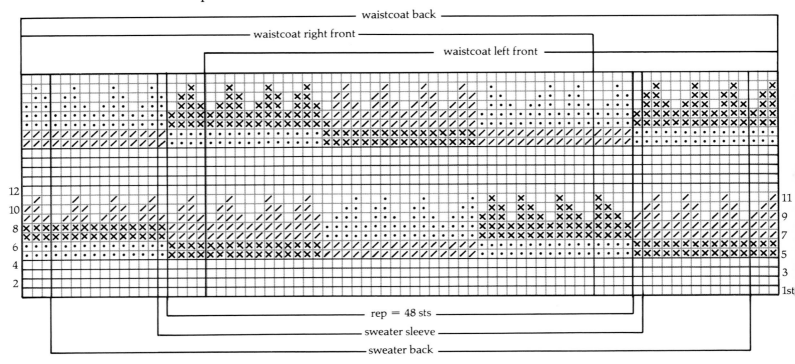

**MEASUREMENTS**
**To fit bust/chest** up to 111cm (44in)
**Actual width** 126cm (49½in)
**Length to shoulder** 71cm (28in)
**Side seam** 47cm (18½in)
**Sleeve seam** 50cm (19½in)

**BACK**
Using 3¾mm (US 5) needles and chosen yarn, cast on 96 sts.
Work 17 rows K1, P1 rib, in stripes at random.
**Next row** Rib 2, K up loop between last st and next st to make 1, (rib 4, make 1) to last 2 sts, rib 2. 120 sts.
Change to 4½mm (US 7) needles and commence colour patt from chart, working in st st throughout beg with a K row, as foll:
**1st–4th rows** Work each row in a different colour.
**5th–8th rows** Work in blocks of 16 sts (12 at each side) in a variety of colours.
**9th–12th rows** Work the 'teeth' in the same colours as previous row but varying the exact shape of them as you please; work the blank squares in the same colour throughout the row. These 12 rows form the patt rep.
Cont in patt until 108 rows have been worked from top of rib, ending with a P row.
**Shape armholes**
Cast off 12 sts at beg of next 2 rows. 96 sts.**
Work 60 rows straight.
**Shape shoulders**
Cast off 11 sts at beg of next 2 rows, then 10 sts at beg of foll 4 rows. 34 sts.
Leave rem sts on a spare needle.

**FRONT**
Work as for back to **.
Work 4 rows straight.
**Divide for neck**
**Next row** Patt 46 sts, K2 tog, turn, leaving rem sts on a spare needle and cont on these sts only for left side of neck. 47 sts.
Work 2 rows. Now dec 1 st at neck edge on next and every foll 3rd row until 31 sts rem.

Now work straight until front matches back to shoulder, ending at armhole edge.
**Shape shoulder**
Cast off 11 sts at beg of next row, then 10 sts at beg of foll alt row. Work 1 row.
Cast off rem 10 sts.
With rs facing rejoin yarn to neck edge, K2 tog tbl, patt to end of row. 47 sts.
Complete right side to match left, reversing shapings.

**SLEEVES**
Using 3¾mm (US 5) needles and chosen yarn, cast on 42 sts.
Work 17 rows K1, P1 rib in stripes as for back.
**Next row** Rib 4, make 1, (rib 5, make 1) to last 3 sts, rib 3. 50 sts.
Change to 4½mm (US 7) needles and work in colour patt as for back, working between sleeve markers on chart, *at the same time* inc 1 st at each end of every foll 5th row until there are 92 sts.
Now work straight until 120 patt rows in all have been completed.
Cast off loosely.

**TO MAKE UP**
Backstitch left shoulder seam.
**Neckband**
Using 3¾mm (US 5) needles and chosen yarn, with rs facing, K across 34 sts of back neck, K up 61 sts down left front neck and 62 sts up right front neck. 157 sts.
Work in K1, P1 rib in stripes as foll:
**1st row** (ws) (P1, K1) 30 times, P2 tog, P2 tog tbl, (K1, P1) to last st, K1. 155 sts.
**2nd row** Rib 92, K2 tog tbl, K2 tog, rib to end.
Cont in this way, work knitwise decs on rs and purlwise decs on ws, rib 6 more rows.
Cast off in rib, dec as before.
Backstitch right shoulder seam.
Set in sleeves flat, matching centre of cast-off edge of sleeve to shoulder seam, and joining last few rows of sleeve to cast-off sts at underarm.
Backstitch side and sleeve seams.

# Waistcoat

## MATERIALS
Approx 300g (11oz) mixed yarns and colours
  averaging four-ply weight
1 pair each 3mm (US 2) and 3¾mm (US 5) needles
6 buttons

## TENSION
26 sts and 33 rows to 10cm (4in) over patt on
3¾mm (US 5) needles.

## MEASUREMENTS
**To fit chest/bust** up to 91cm (36in)
**Actual width** 96cm (38in)
**Length to shoulder** 48cm (18½in)
**Side seam** 28cm (11in)

## BACK
Using 3mm (US 2) needles and chosen yarn, cast
on 126 sts. Work 9 rows st st, beg with a K row.
K 1 row to form hemline.
Change to 3¾mm (US 5) needles and commence
colour patt as shown on chart on page 36,
working between markers for waistcoat back, rep
3rd–12th rows only and foll guidelines given for
sweater back; work 94 rows, beg with a K row.
**Shape armholes**
Cast off 6 sts at beg of next 2 rows, then 3 sts at
beg of foll 2 rows and 2 sts at beg of foll 4 rows.
Now dec 1 st at each end of next and foll 2 alt
rows. 94 sts. Now work straight until 160 patt
rows in all have been worked, ending with a ws
row.
**Shape shoulders**
Cast off 8 sts at beg of next 6 rows. Leave rem 46
sts on a spare needle.

## LEFT FRONT
Using 3mm (US 2) needles and yarn as for back,
cast on 59 sts. Work 9 rows st st, beg with a K
row. K 1 row to form hemline.
Change to 3¾mm (US 5) needles and cont in
colour patt as for back, working between left
front markers on chart, until work measures 14
rows less than back to underarm, end with a P row.
**Shape front**
Cont in patt, dec 1 st at end of next and every foll
4th row until 55 sts rem, ending with a K row.
Work 1 row.
**Shape armhole**
Cast off 6 sts at beg of next row, then 3 sts at beg
of foll alt row, and 2 sts at beg of next 2 alt rows,
then dec 1 st at beg of foll 3 alt rows, *at the same
time* cont to dec at front edge on every 4th row as
before until 24 sts rem. Work straight until front
matches back to shoulder, end with a P row.
**Shape shoulder**
Cast off 8 sts at beg of next and foll alt row. Work
1 row. Cast off rem 8 sts.

## RIGHT FRONT
Work as given for left front, working between
right front markers on chart, reversing shapings.

## TO MAKE UP
Backstitch shoulder seams.
**Armhole edges**
Using 3mm (US 2) needles and chosen yarn, with

Toothed stripe

**Front band chart**

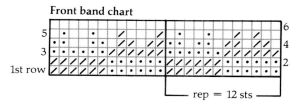

rep = 12 sts

rs facing K up 144 sts round armhole edge. P 2
rows for foldline. Work 4 rows st st, beg with a P
row. Cast off loosely.
Join side seams.
Fold all hems on to ws and catch down.
**Front band**
Using 3¾mm (US 5) needles and chosen yarn,
with rs facing K up 324 sts all round front edge.
Work in st st, beg with a P row, foll colour patt
from front band chart, work 1st–6th rows,
making buttonholes on 3rd and 4th rows as foll:
**1st buttonhole row** Patt 2 sts, (cast off 2, patt 10
including st used to cast off) 6 times, patt to end.
**2nd buttonhole row** Patt to end casting on 2 sts
over those cast off in previous row.
When chart is completed change to 3mm (US 2)
needles. P 2 rows to form foldline.
Work 4 rows st st beg with a P row. Work 2
buttonhole rows as before. Work 8 rows st st, beg
with a P row. Cast off loosely.
Neaten buttonholes. Sew on buttons.

(Overleaf) *In Malta, the
Toothed Stripe Waistcoat
in my original bright
pastels scheme echoing the
colours of a rag rug in
progress.*

(Below) *The Toothed
Waistcoat in a rich array
of jewel blues and
turquoises in front of a
truckful of cut tulip heads
in the Keukenhof Gardens
in Holland.*

# Carpet Pattern

Years ago I bought a kilim with this design just so that I could copy it (see page 83). Since then I've used it many times over in jackets, coats and pullovers. I used it first on a large scale, and I've returned to it time and again because of the wonderful way it takes colour.

The coat (page 42) is in chunky yarns worked on large needles, so it can be knitted up quickly. In spite of the apparent intricacy of the design, the colours are actually worked in fairly large areas.

The pattern is worked by the intarsia method (the yarns are twisted together at each colour change, rather than being carried across the back, though you can weave them in in some places to ensure the yarn is in the correct position for the next row).

Pick out groups of colours which harmonize but contrast enough to show the pattern layout. Keep some colours going for several rows and others for short 'shots' (use manageable lengths for the latter). There are basically two ways of working this design: either use two groups of colours, one deeper and one lighter, so that the contrast between them will show up the structure of the pattern strongly, or use very close tones for a tweedy look, all but losing the structure.

(Far right) *We found some wonderful locations in Malta. These for the Carpet Pullover are two of my favourites. The main picture was taken in a deserted villa against a background of weathered painted walls. We spotted the old ladies in the inset picture, veiled by a mosquito screen, in a small village. Their dress prints toned so perfectly with the beiges of the pullover.*

## Pullover

Looking at old weathered wooden doors and faded winter leaves encouraged me to believe that hundreds of shades of grey and pale beige-browns would make a subtle and attractive colouring. There are at least sixty colours in this rather neat sleeveless pullover. It is a case of collecting as many washed out, natural tones of beiges and blue-greys as you can find and setting to work. This is a particularly good example of how the structure of the pattern can be almost lost when you're using close colours.

MATERIALS
Approx 300g (11oz) mixed yarns and colours in two distinct tonal ranges (A, B) averaging four-ply weight
1 pair each 3mm (US 2) and 3¾mm (US 5) needles

TENSION
21 sts and 32 rows to 10cm (4in) over patt on 3¾mm (US 5) needles.

MEASUREMENTS
**To fit bust/chest** up to 101cm (40in)
**Actual width** 110cm (43in)
**Length to shoulder** 60cm (23½in)
**Side seam** 36cm (14in)

BACK
Using 3mm (US 2) needles and chosen yarn, cast on 114 sts.
Work 20 rows K1, P1 rib in stripes at random, inc 1 st at each end of last row. 116 sts.
Change to 3¾mm (US 5) needles and commence colour patt from chart, working in st st throughout and twisting yarns between colours to avoid holes, as foll:
**1st row** (rs) K2A, (11A, 34B, 11A) twice, 2A.
**2nd row** P2A, (10A, 36B, 10A) twice, 2A.
Cont in patt as set, changing to different colours in the A and B group as required, rep 1st–72nd chart rows until 100 rows in all have been worked in colour patt, ending with a ws row.
**Shape armholes**
Cast off 6 sts at beg of next 2 rows, then 2 sts at beg of foll 8 rows. 88 sts.** Now dec 1 st at each end of next and foll 5 alt rows, and then at each end of 2 foll 4th rows. 72 sts.
Work straight until 176 rows in all have been worked in colour patt, ending with a ws row.
**Shape shoulders**
Cast off 7 sts at beg of next 2 rows and 6 sts at beg of foll 4 rows. 34 sts.
Leave these sts on a spare needle.

FRONT
Work as given for back to **.
**Divide for neck**
**Next row** (rs) K2 tog, patt 40 sts, K2 tog, K2 tog tbl, patt to last 2 sts, K2 tog.
**Next row** Patt 42 sts, turn, leaving rem sts on a spare needle and cont on these sts only for right front.

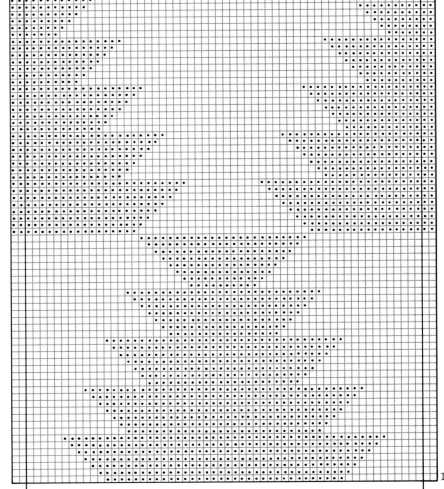

72

1st row

rep = 56 sts

**Key** □ = A  ⊡ = B

40

Stripes

Dec 1 st at armhole edge on next and foll 4 alt rows, then on 2 foll 4th rows, *at the same time* dec 1 st at neck edge on 3rd and every foll 4th row until 19 sts rem.

Work straight until front matches back to shoulder, ending at armhole edge.

**Shape shoulder**
Cast off 7 sts at beg of next row and 6 sts at beg of foll alt row.
Work 1 row. Cast off rem 6 sts. With ws facing rejoin yarn to neck edge, patt to end of row, then complete left side to match right, reversing shapings.

TO MAKE UP
Backstitch left shoulder seam.
**Neckband**
Using 3mm (US 2) needles and chosen yarn, with rs facing K 34 sts across back neck, K up 68 sts down left front neck and 69 sts up right front neck. 171 sts.
Work in K1, P1 rib in stripes as for back rib as foll:
**1st row** (ws) (K1,P1) 33 times, K1, P2 tog, P2 tog tbl, (K1, P1) to end. 169 sts.
**2nd row** Rib 99, K2 tog tbl, K2 tog, rib to end. 167 sts.
Cont to dec in this way, working knitwise decs on rs rows and purlwise decs on ws rows, rib 7 more rows. 153 sts.
Cast off in rib, dec as before.
Backstitch right shoulder seam.
**Armbands**
Using 3mm (US 2) needles and chosen yarn, with rs facing K up 170 sts around armhole edge.
P 1 row, then K 2 rows to form foldline.
Work 4 rows st st, beg with a K row.
Cast off loosely.
Backstitch side seams. Fold armbands on to ws and catch down.

# Coat

The Carpet Coat (see page 44) was designed for someone who loves muted colours. She wanted a glorious coat that wasn't too dramatic ('so it won't wear me'). I kept the colours fairly close in value so the contrasts wouldn't be too loud—greys, browns, soft rusts and a touch of mossy green. There are about sixty colours in this coat—some are plied wool and mohair combinations; it reminds me a lot of the colours of the California coast where I was brought up.

MATERIALS
Approx 1650g (59oz) mixed yarns and colours in two distinct tonal ranges (A,B) averaging chunky weight
1 pair each 5mm (US 8) and 6mm (US 10) needles

TENSION
14 sts and 20 rows to 10cm (4in) over patt on 6mm (US 10) needles.

MEASUREMENTS
**To fit bust/chest** up to 111cm (44in)
**Actual width** 217cm (85½in)
**Length to shoulder** 108cm (45½in)
**Side seam** 83cm (33in)
**Sleeve seam** 31cm (12in)

BACK, FRONT AND SLEEVES (one piece)
Beg at lower back edge, using 5mm (US 8) needles and chosen yarn, cast on 76 sts.
Work 15 rows K1, P1 rib in stripes at random.
**Next row** (Work into front and back of each st) to end. 152 sts.
Change to 6mm (US 10) needles and commence colour patt from chart 1, working in st st throughout and twisting yarns between colours to avoid holes, as foll:
**1st row** (rs) K9A, 56B, 22A, 56B, 9A.
**2nd row** P8A, 58B, 20A, 58B, 8A.
Cont in patt as set, working first half of each row reading from right to left on chart 1 and second half of each row reversing the chart by reading left to right (left half of coat is a mirror image of right half), rep 1st–80th rows until 148 patt rows in all have been worked, ending with a ws row (mark each end of 100th and 130th rows for pockets).
**Shape sleeves**
Cast on 25 sts at beg of next 2 rows. 202 sts.
Cont in patt, working from chart 1 for body, chart 2 for right sleeve and reversing chart 2 for left sleeve, work straight until 198 patt rows in all have been completed, ending with a ws row.
**Divide for neck and fronts**
**Next row** Patt 93 sts, turn, leaving rem sts on a spare needle and cont on these sts only for right side of neck.
Cast off 6 sts at beg of next row. (This point marks the shoulder line, reverse patt from this point.)** Dec 1 st at beg of foll alt row. Work 7 rows straight ending at neck edge. Inc 1 st at beg of next and foll alt row, then cast on 2 sts at beg of next alt row, 4 sts at beg of foll alt row and 7sts at beg of foll alt row. 101 sts.
Work straight until front sleeve matches back sleeve from shoulder line, ending at sleeve edge.
**Shape sleeve**
Cast off 25 sts at beg of next row. 76 sts.
Now work straight until front matches back from shoulder line to top of rib, marking equivalent rows on side edge for pocket.
Change to 5mm (US 8) needles and yarn as for back rib.
**Next row** (Work 2 tog) to end. 38 sts.
Work 15 rows K1, P1 rib in stripes at random.
Cast off in rib.
With rs facing rejoin yarn to neck edge, cast off 16 sts, patt to end. 93 sts.
Work 1 row. (This point marks the shoulder line, reverse patt from this point.) Cast off 6 sts at beg of next row. Complete left side to match right, working from ** to end.

LEFT POCKET LINING
Using 6mm (US 10) needles and chosen yarn, with rs facing K up 25 sts between pocket markers on left back side edge.
Work in st st beg with a P row, cast on 8 sts at beg of next row. Work 3 rows. Dec 1 st at end of next and every foll alt row until 20 sts rem.
Cast off.

RIGHT POCKET LINING
Work as for left pocket lining working between markers on right back side and reversing shapings.

## POCKET EDGINGS

Using 5mm (US 8) needles and chosen yarn, with rs facing K up 25 sts between pocket markers on fronts.
K 1 row to form foldline. Work 6 rows st st beg with a K row.
Cast off loosely.

## CUFFS

Using 5mm (US 8) needles and yarn as for back rib, with rs facing K up 51 sts along sleeve edge.
Work 4 rows K1, P1 rib.
**Next row** Work 2 tog, (rib 8, work 2 tog) to last 9 sts, rib to end. 46 sts.
Work 4 rows K1, P1 rib.
**Next row** Work 2 tog, rib 6, work 2 tog, (rib 7, work 2 tog) to end. 40 sts.
Work 4 rows K1, P1 rib.
**Next row** Work 2 tog, rib 5, work 2 tog, (rib 6, work 2 tog) to last 7 sts, rib to end. 35 sts.
Work 4 rows K1, P1 rib.
**Next row** Rib 6, work 2 tog, (rib 5, work 2 tog) to last 6 sts, rib 6. 31 sts.
Work 3 rows K1, P1 rib.
Cast off in rib.

## FRONT BANDS (alike)

Using 5mm (US 8) needles and chosen yarn, with rs facing K up 168 sts up front edge. K 1 row to form foldline.
Work 12 rows st st, beg with a K row.
Cast off loosely.

## TO MAKE UP

Fold front bands on to ws and catch down.
**Collar**
Using 5mm (US 8) needles and yarn as for front bands, with rs facing K up 90 sts around neck edge.
Work 9 rows K1, P1 rib.
**Next row** Rib 1, (work 2 tog, rib 10) to last 5 sts, work 2 tog, rib to end. 82 sts.
Work 7 rows K1, P1 rib.
**Next row** Rib 2, (work 2 tog, rib 9) to last 3 sts, work 2 tog, rib 1. 74 sts.
Work 5 rows K1, P1 rib.
**Next row** Rib 1, work 2 tog, (rib 8, work 2 tog) to last st, rib 1. 66 sts.
Work 5 rows K1, P1 rib.
**Next row** Rib 1, (work 2 tog, rib 7) to last 2 sts, work 2 tog. 58 sts.
Rib 1 row.
Cast off in rib.
Fold pocket edgings on to ws and catch down.
Join side and sleeve seams. Catch down pocket linings on to ws of fronts.

(Overleaf) *It's amazing how a background can affect colours. A pea green door and cool jade green bridge bring out two very different aspects of the Carpet Coat.*

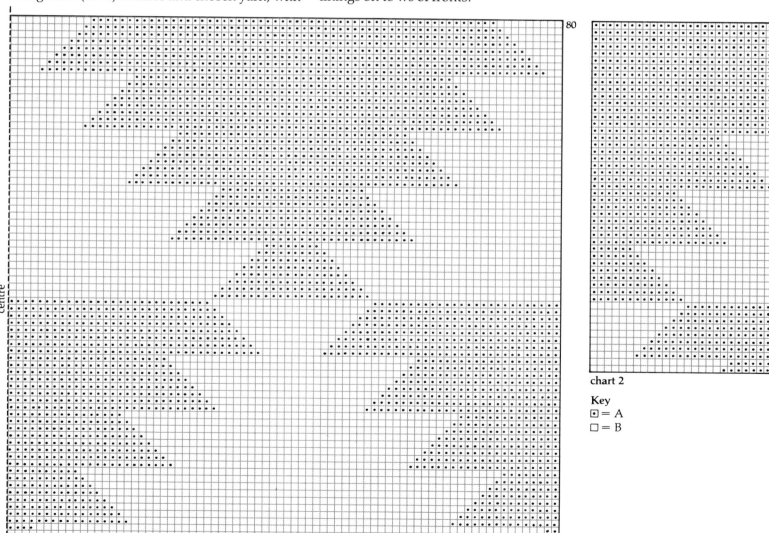

chart 1

chart 2

**Key**
⊡ = A
□ = B

# STEPS & ZIGZAGS

lthough steps can suggest the solidity of architecture, there is often a definite feeling of movement to the design as it progresses up or across a garment. The regularity and simple straight lines of these two motifs make them technically easy to accomplish in many different mediums, so both have been firm favourites with artists, craftsmen and craftswomen for thousands of years.

In primitive art steps and zigzags are often used to suggest thunder and lightning. The stepped forms found on Mexican rugs and embroideries and on Peruvian textiles (including knitted fabrics) may well be an echo of the magnificent stepped pyramids and temples of their Mayan and Inca ancestors.

In more recent times, both steps and zigzags found favour with artists of the Art Deco movement, who often took their inspiration from things like African beadwork and Indian basketry. These stark geometric forms in a riot of glorious colour can be found on many objects of that period throughout the world—fabrics, ceramics, wallpaper, furniture, and also in architectural details like doors, windows, light fittings and so on.

Being essentially very simple motifs, they are ideal for lots of experiments with scale and placement (they also lend themselves to endless colour and mood variations). You'll see something of what I mean in the step variations in the following pages, but try this simple exercise for yourself. Draw a dozen sweater shapes on a large sheet of paper. Take a theme—squares, parasols, pots of flowers, steps—and draw it in different scales and positions on your shapes. You'll soon find out how many different approaches you can take, and how even simple changes in scale and placement can make a dramatic difference.

*This shawl* (far left) *is a perfect example of the games you can play with placing motifs, and the step pattern is the perfect candidate for a freewheeling approach. I began one of my usual triangular shawls with an inverted Small Steps layout then started another series of steps half-way up at each side. By the way, these shawls make colourful furnishings, thrown over couches, hung on walls or covering the backs of large easy chairs (which makes them nicely to hand for wrapping up chilly looking guests).*

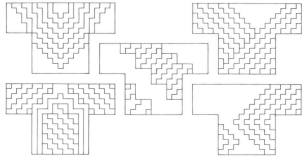

47

# Small Steps

The progression of this pattern is fascinating. It almost seems to have a life of its own. Each stepped stripe is four stitches wide and four rows deep, and there are eight rows straight between each bend in the 'staircase'. Once you get going on it, you hardly need to consult the chart. Just carry on merrily knitting and, if you make a mistake (as I frequently do), don't worry too much about it. The design is so strong that, in most cases, it will look perfectly balanced whatever you do. Anyway, if you do allow it to meander a little, you will have a garment that is unique—nobody meanders in quite the same direction as anybody else.

## Crew-neck Sweater

The version specified in the pattern was made for the autumn with golds and earthy dead leaf colours. I used fine tweed yarns run together (pink or grey with gold) as well as Aran-weight tweeds and plain wools. This design is a natural for many colour experiments, whether soft and muted or dramatically contrasting. I've also done one with a slightly different step layout in deep tweedy shades (see page 50).

MATERIALS
**Yarn used**
100[125,150]g (4[5,6]oz) Rowan Spun Tweed in caviar 760 (A); 100[100:150]g (4[4,6]oz) each in tobacco 751 (B), fig 761 (C) and caper 762 (D)
75[75,100]g (3[3,4]oz) Rowan Yarns Light Tweed in charcoal 210 (L); 50[75,100]g (2[3,4]oz) in rosemix 215 (G); 50[50,75]g (2[2,3]oz) each in bamboo 218 (E), autumn 205 (H) and jungle 212 (J); 25g (1oz) in grey 209 (F)
75[75,100]g (3[3,4]oz) Rowan Yarns Double Knitting Wool in light tan 9 (M)
**Equivalent yarn** Aran/medium-weight
1 pair each 3¾mm (US 5) and 4½mm (US 7) needles

NOTE
*The finer yarns (E–M) are used in combination. For example, 'EG' means one strand each of yarns E and G; 'LL' means two strands of yarn L. If preferred Aran or medium-weight yarns used singly may be substituted for the combined yarns throughout.*

TENSION
18 sts and 25 rows to 10cm (4in) over patt on 4½mm (US 7) needles.

MEASUREMENTS
**To fit bust/chest** 91[96,101]cm (36[38,40]in)
**Actual width** 102[111,120]cm (40[44,47]in)
**Length to shoulder** 60[61,62]cm (23½[24,24½]in)
**Side seam** 37cm (14½in)
**Sleeve seam** 41[41,42]cm (16[16,16½]in)

BACK
Using 3¾mm (US 5) needles and yarn A, cast on 78[86,94] sts. Work in K1, P1 rib as foll: 4 rows in B, 4 rows in A, 4 rows in C, 3 rows in LL.

(Far right) *The autumn colouring (given in the pattern) for the Small Steps Crew-neck Sweater, photographed in Westonbirt Arboretum near Tetbury, Gloucestershire. The coat (inset) gives you an extra idea to try for yourself. I used a step motif somewhere in scale between Small Steps and Large Steps on a basic kimono coat shape made all in one piece, and essentially a longer version of the Large Diamond Jacket on page 68. It's worn over the Small Steps Crew-neck Sweater.*

# Steps & Zigzags

**Next row** With yarns LL, rib 6[4,1], K up loop between next st and last st to make 1, (rib 5[6,7], make 1) to last 7[4,2] sts, rib to end of row. 92[100,108] sts.
Change to 4½mm (US 7) needles and, working in st st throughout beg with a K row, commence colour patt from chart, twist yarns between colours to avoid holes (do not carry yarns across the back), as foll:
**1st row** (rs) K4D[8D,(4EG,8D)], 4JM, 4A, 8EF, 4B, 4EG, 8D, 4JM, 4A, 4C, 4A, 4JM, 8D, 4EG, 4B, 8EF, 4A, 4JM, 4D[8D,(8D,4EG)].
**2nd and every foll alt row** P to end using same colours as in previous row.
Cont in patt as set, working each step line in the same colour throughout, introducing a new step line in a new colour every 16th row and losing one of the original step lines at the sides at the same time, as shown on chart. Work 78 rows without shaping, ending with a P row.

*The Large Steps Jacket and the dark tweedy Small Steps Crew-neck toning beautifully with a wonderful Dutch door aged from deep navy to this metallic plum tone.*

### Shape armholes
Cast off 10 sts at beg of next 2 rows. 72[80,88] sts.
Work 56[58,60] rows without shaping, ending with a P row.
### Shape shoulder and divide for neck
**Next row** Cast off 7[8,9] sts, patt 21[24,27] sts, cast off 16 sts, patt to end.
**Next row** Cast off 7[8,9] sts, patt to neck edge, turn, leaving rem sts on a spare needle and cont on these sts only for the left side of the neck. 21[24,27] sts.
Cast off 5 sts at beg of next row, 7[8,9] sts at beg of foll row and 4 sts at beg of foll row.
Cast off rem 5[7,9] sts.
With ws facing rejoin yarn to right side neck edge and complete to match left side, reversing shapings.

FRONT
Work as given for back until 112[114,116] patt rows have been worked, ending with a P row.
### Divide for neck
**Next row** Patt 31[35,39] sts, cast off 10 sts, patt to end of row.
**Next row** Patt to neck edge, turn, leaving rem sts on a spare needle and cont on these sts only for right side of neck. 31[35,39] sts.
Cast off 3 sts at beg of next row and 2 sts at beg of foll 2 alt rows.
Now dec 1 st at the neck edge on the foll 5 alt rows. 19[23,27] sts.
Work straight until front matches back to shoulder shaping, ending at armhole edge.
### Shape shoulder
Cast off 7[8,9] sts at beg of next and foll alt row.
Work 1 row.
Cast off rem 5[7,9] sts.
With ws facing rejoin yarn to sts at left neck edge and complete to match right side, reversing shapings.

SLEEVES
Using 3¾mm (US 5) needles and yarn A, cast on 38[40,42] sts.
Work 15 rows K1, P1 rib as given for back.
**Next row** With yarns LL, rib 5[3,4], make 1, (rib 4[5,5], make 1) to last 5[2,3] sts, rib to end. 46[48,50] sts.
Change to 4½mm (US 7) needles and commence patt from chart, working between sleeve markers, *at the same time* inc 1 st at each end of 5th and every foll 4th row until there are 82[86,90] sts on needle.
Now work straight until 100[100,104] patt rows have been worked.
Cast off loosely.

TO MAKE UP
Backstitch left shoulder seam.
### Neckband
Using 3¾mm (US 5) needles and yarns LL, with rs of work facing, K up 40 sts round back neck and 68 sts round front neck. 108 sts.
Work 8 rows K1, P1 rib as foll: 1 row in LL, 2 rows in C, 2 rows in A, 2 rows in B, 1 row in A.
Cast off in rib in A.
Backstitch right shoulder seam.
Set sleeves in flat using a backstitch seam.
Backstitch side and sleeve seams.

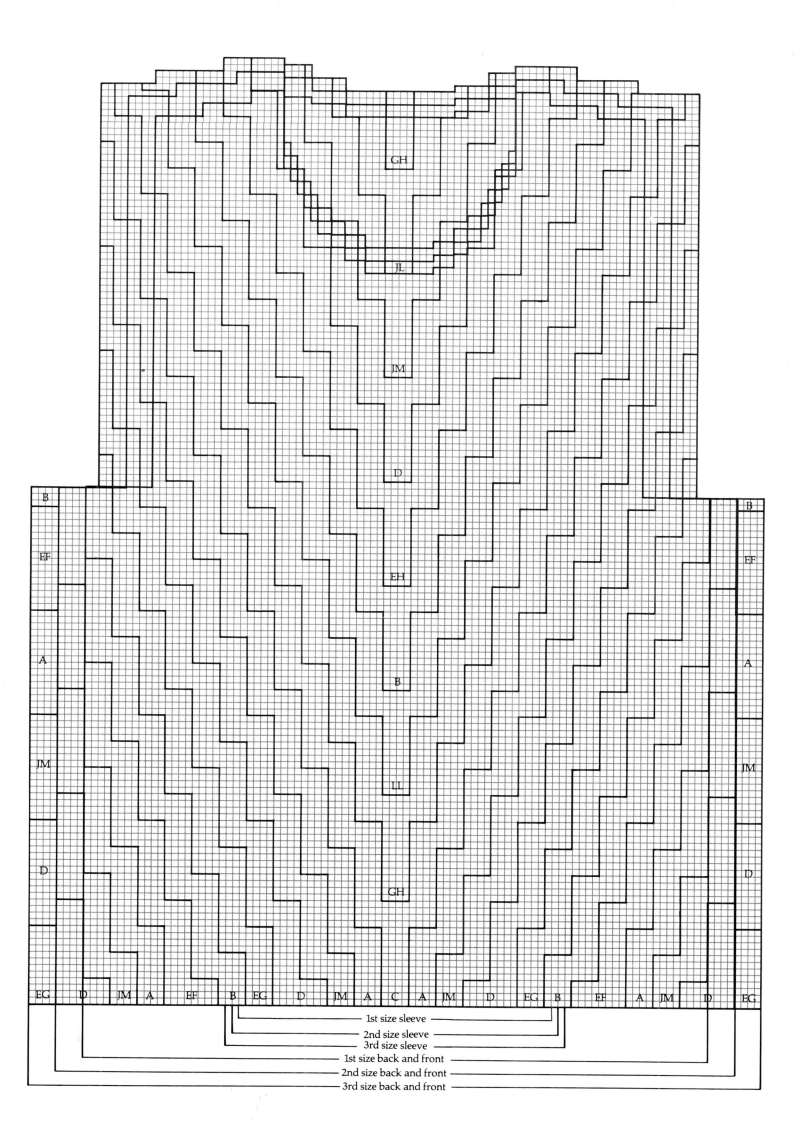

GH

JL

JM

D

B

EF

A

JM

D

EG

B

EF

A

JM

D

EG

EH

B

LL

GH

EG | D | JM | A | EF | B | EG | D | JM | A | C | A | JM | D | EG | B | EF | A | JM | D | EG

1st size sleeve
2nd size sleeve
3rd size sleeve
1st size back and front
2nd size back and front
3rd size back and front

# V-neck Sweater

This design was originally meant to be a very fancy waistcoat for a man to wear under a dinner jacket. I was thinking of dark Chinese silk brocades where the shiny bronzes and silver threads add a special deep glow to the colouring. Then a woman friend bagged the colour layout for a V-neck puff-sleeved shape and it worked superbly well. This shape would, in fact, work well with many different patterns and colourings—the Lattice or Ribbon designs (pages 118 and 110), for example. The Little Squares version (see page 123) just uses every shade of gold and copper you can lay your hands on, knitted into five-stitch by five-row squares.

The midnight scheme would be a good starting point for other garments too. The trick with dark colourings is to get them dark enough. If your colours aren't quite dark enough, twist a thin black or dark brown in with them. You could try the waistcoat idea, if you can find a man daring enough to wear it!

## MATERIALS
Approx 375[450]g (14[16]oz) mixed yarns averaging double knitting weight in at least 10 colours (A, B, C, D, E, F, G, H, J, L, etc)
1 pair each 3¼mm (US 3) and 4mm (US 6) needles
1 set four double-pointed 3¼mm (US 3) needles (or circular needle)

## TENSION
22 sts and 30 rows to 10cm (4in) over patt on 4mm (US 6) needles.

## MEASUREMENTS
**To fit bust** 76–81[86–91]cm (30–32[34–36]in)
**Actual width** 84[95]cm (33[37]in)
**Length to shoulder** 47[51]cm (18[19½]in)
**Side seam** 32cm (12in)
**Sleeve seam** 41[43]cm (16[17]in)

## BACK
Using 3¼mm (US 3) needles and chosen colour, cast on 86[98] sts.
Work 20 rows K1, P1 rib in stripes at random.
Change to 4mm (US 6) needles. Work in st st, commence colour patt from chart, twisting yarns between colours to avoid holes (do not carry yarns across the back), as foll:
**1st row** (rs) K1[7]A, 4B, 4C, 8D, 4E, 4F, 8G, 4H, 4J, 4G, 4J, 4H, 8G, 4F, 4E, 8D, 4C, 4B, 1[7]A.

**2nd and every foll alt row** P to end using same colours as in previous row.
Cont in patt as set rep 1st–16th rows, working each step line in the same colour throughout and introducing new colours (or rep an original colour) for a new step line every 16th row, *at the same time* inc 1 st at each end of 21st, and 2 foll 20th rows, working the extra sts into patt, work 78 patt rows in all, end with a ws row. 92[104] sts.
**Shape armholes**
Cast off 7 sts at beg of next 2 rows, then dec 1 st at each end of foll 6 alt rows. 66[78] sts.
Now work straight until 124[136] patt rows in all have been worked, ending with a ws row.
**Shape shoulders and divide for neck**
**Next row** Cast off 5[7] sts, patt 21[23] sts, cast off 14[18] sts, patt to end.
**Next row** Cast off 5[7] sts, patt to neck edge, turn, leaving rem sts on a spare needle and cont on these sts only for left side of neck. 21[23] sts.
Cast off 9 sts at beg of next row and 6[7] sts at beg of foll row. Work 1 row. Cast off rem 6[7] sts.
With ws facing, rejoin yarn to neck edge and complete right side to match left, reversing shapings.

## FRONT
Work as given for back until 70 patt rows in all have been worked from chart, ending with a ws row.
**Divide for neck**
**Next row** Patt 44[50] sts, K2 tog, K2 tog tbl, patt to end.
**Next row** Patt to neck edge, turn, leaving rem sts on a spare needle and cont on these sts only for right side of neck. 45[51] sts.
Cont in patt, dec 1 st at neck edge on 2 foll 3rd rows. Work 2 rows straight, thus ending at armhole edge.
**Shape armhole**
Cast off 7 sts at beg of next row, then dec 1 st at armhole edge on foll 6 alt rows, *at the same time* cont to dec at neck edge on every 3rd row from previous dec until 17[21] sts rem. Cont without shaping until front matches back to shoulder, ending at armhole edge.
**Shape shoulder**
Cast off 5[7] sts at beg of next row and 6[7] sts at beg of foll alt row. Work 1 row. Cast off.
With ws of work facing, rejoin yarn to neck edge. Cont in patt, dec 1 st at neck edge on 2 foll 3rd rows. Work 1 row straight, thus ending at armhole edge. Complete to match right side.

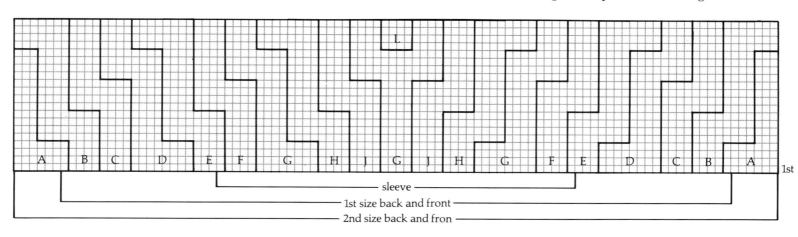

A    B    C    D    E    F    G    H    I    G    J    H    G    F    E    D    C    B    A    1st

sleeve
1st size back and front
2nd size back and fron

52

*The symmetrical placing of the step lines describes the shape of the body and sleeve quite perfectly. For a complete contrast of mood try it in delicate, mother-of-pearl shades.*

## Neckband

Using 3¼mm (US 3) double-pointed needles and chosen yarn, with rs facing, K up 33[35] sts across back neck, 60[70] sts down left side of neck and 60[70] sts up right side of neck. 153[175] sts.
Work in K1, P1 rib as foll:
**1st round** Rib 91[103], K2 tog tbl, K2 tog, (P1, K1) to end.
**2nd round** Rib 90[102], K2 tog tbl, K2 tog, (K1, P1) to end.
Cont to dec at centre front working knitwise decs on every round, work 6 rounds.
Cast off, dec as before at centre front.

## SLEEVES

Using 3¼mm (US 3) needles and yarn as for back rib, cast on 46 sts. Work 20 rows, K1, P1 rib as for back.
Change to 4mm (US 6) needles and commence colour patt from chart, in colours as for back,

working between sleeve markers, *at the same time* inc 1 st at each end of 9th and every foll 8th row until there are 62[56] sts.
Now inc 1 st at each end of every foll 4th row until there are 76[82] sts, and then at each end of every alt row until there are 86[92] sts. Work 2 rows.

### Shape top

Cast off 7 sts at beg of next 2 rows, then dec 1 st at each end of 10[13] foll 4th rows. 52 sts.
Dec 1 st at each end of every alt row until 40 sts rem, ending with a P row.
**Next row** (K2 tog) to end. 20 sts.
Cast off.

## TO MAKE UP

Backstitch shoulder seams.
Backstitch sleeves into armholes, making three pleats on each side of shoulder seam. Backstitch side and sleeve seams.

# Large Steps

This is the sort of scale I really enjoy, big and bold! The huge dynamic forms move dramatically up the garment, softened by the colour changes within each step line. For the most striking look, make these designs in only two colours or use much closer tones within the two contrasting sections to emphasize their silhouettes.

The large areas of colour make this design very quick and enjoyable to knit.

## Jacket

These dark smouldering colours on a bold cutting design seem to be universally appealing. It certainly looks great on men and women. I used raw silk, chunky tweeds, cotton chenille, and mohair mixed with wool. The blue version uses the same textures as the maroon but with a blue and black cast with sage green undertones, and was largely inspired by Chinese work clothes.

MATERIALS
Approx 1250g (44oz) total weight in mixed chunky yarns in 2 colours or groups of colours (A,B)
1 pair each 4½mm (US 7), 5½mm (US 9) and 6½mm (US 10½) needles
8 buttons

TENSION
14 sts and 19 rows to 10cm (4in) over patt on 6½mm needles.

MEASUREMENTS
**To fit bust/chest** up to 111cm (44in)
**Actual width** 137cm (54in)
**Length to shoulder** 75cm (29½in)
**Side seam** 44cm (17½in)
**Sleeve seam** 38cm (15in)

BACK AND FRONTS (one piece)
Beg at lower edge back, using 5½mm (US 9) needles and chosen yarn, cast on 78 sts.
Work 12 rows K1, P1 rib.
**Next row** Rib 5, K up loop between next st and last st to make 1, (rib 4, make 1) to last 5 sts, rib 5. 96 sts.
Change to 6½mm (US 10½) needles and, working in st st beg with a K row, commence colour patt from chart 1 (page 56), twist yarns together between colours (do not carry yarns across the back).
**1st row** (rs) K (12A, 24B) twice, 12A, 12B.
**2nd and every foll alt row** P to end using same colours or groups of colours as previous row.
Cont in patt as set, rep 1st–84th rows working each stepline in same colour or group of colours throughout, until 130 patt rows in all have been worked, ending with a P row (mark each end of 10th and 43rd rows for pockets).
**Divide for fronts**
**131st row** Patt 44 sts, cast off 8 sts, patt to end.
**132nd row** Patt to neck edge, turn, leaving rem sts on a spare needle and cont on these sts only for left front. 44 sts.

*This bank of high magenta blooms is a sympathetic ground for both the blue and the maroon colourways of the Large Steps Jacket. See the front of the blue version opposite the title page. The jackets are large and roomy but they seem to hang well on practically anybody.*

## Steps & Zigzags

**Shape neck**
Keeping patt correct, foll chart 2 to reverse patt at shoulder line, *at the same time* cast off 4 sts at beg of next row and 1 st at beg of foll alt row. 39 sts.
Work 5 rows straight, ending with a P row.
Now cast on 1 st at beg of next and 2 foll alt rows, then 2 sts at beg of foll alt row and 4 sts at beg of next alt row. 48 sts.
Now work straight, cont to reverse chart patt as before until 133 rows have been worked from shoulder line, marking side edge on same rows as on back for pockets.
Change to 5½mm (US 9) needles and same yarn as used for back rib.
**Next row** K1, P1, K1, (P2 tog, K1, P1, K1) to end. 39 sts.
Work 12 rows K1, P1 rib as set.
Cast off in rib.
With ws facing, using 6½mm (US 10½) needles,

rejoin yarn to right neck edge and complete right front to match left front, reversing shapings and foll chart 2 to reverse colour patt at shoulder line.

### SLEEVES
Using 5½mm (US 9) needles and chosen yarn, cast on 32 sts.
Work 12 rows K1, P1 rib.
Change to 6½mm (US 10½) needles and commence colour patt from chart working between sleeve markers, *at the same time* inc 1 st at each end of 3rd and every foll alt row until there are 86 sts.
Now work straight until 62 patt rows in all have been worked.
Cast off loosely.

### RIGHT POCKET LINING
Using 6½mm (US 10½) needles and chosen yarn,

chart 1

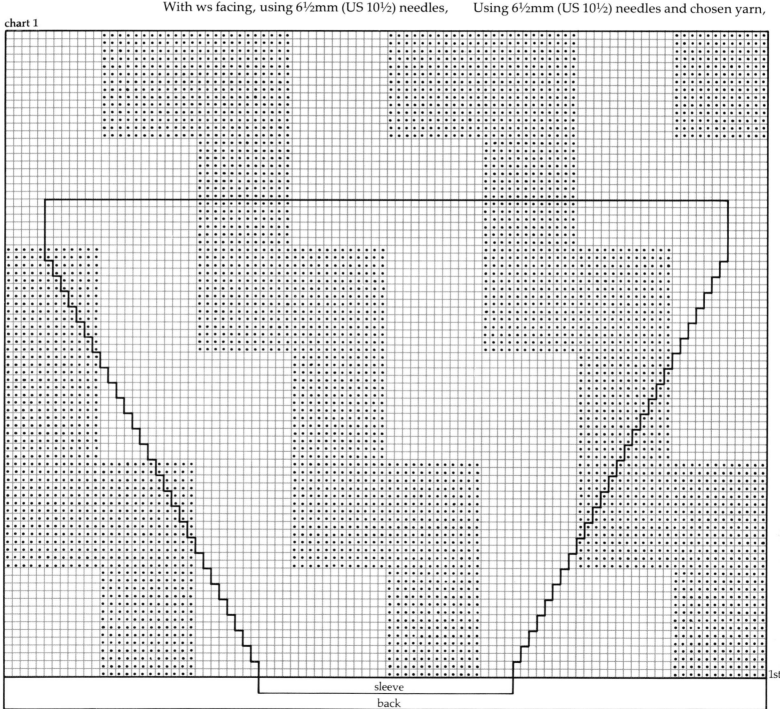

sleeve
back

**Key** ⊡ = A  ☐ = B

with rs of work facing, K up 26 sts between pocket markers on right side back edge. P 1 row. Cont in st st, cast on 4 sts at beg of next row. 30 sts. Now dec 1 st at beg of next and every foll P row until 17 sts rem.
Cast off.

## LEFT POCKET LINING
Using 6½mm (US 10½) needles and chosen yarn, with rs facing, K up 26 sts between pocket markers on left side back edge.
Work in st st beg with a P row, cast on 4 sts at beg of next row. 30 sts.
Now dec 1 st at beg of next and every foll K row until 17 sts rem.
Cast off.

## POCKET EDGINGS
Using 5½mm (US 9) needles and chosen yarn, with rs of work facing, K up 26 sts between pocket markers on left front side edge (for left pocket and right front side edge for right pocket).
K 1 row to form foldline.
Work 4 rows st st beg with a K row.
Cast off loosely.

## TO MAKE UP
Sew sleeves in flat using a backstitch seam, matching centre of cast-off edge to shoulder line.
Fold pocket edgings on to ws of work and catch down.
Backstitch side and sleeve seams.
Catch down pocket linings to ws of fronts.
**Button band**
Using 5½mm (US 9) needles and chosen yarn, with rs facing K up 104 sts (10 sts across rib and 94 sts on main part) along right front edge (for a man's jacket, left front edge for a woman's).
P 1 row, then K 2 rows to form foldline.
Change to 4½mm (US 7) needles and work 8 rows st st, beg with a K row.
Cast off loosely.
**Buttonhole band**
K up sts along second front edge as given for button band, *at the same time* make buttonholes on K up row as foll:
**K up and buttonhole row** K up 3 sts, *K up 2 sts, lift 2nd st on right-hand needle over 1st st and off needle, K up 1 st, lift 2nd st on right-hand needle over 1st st and off needle, K up 11; rep from * 8 times, ending last rep K up 2.
**Next row** P to end, casting on 2 sts over those cast off in previous row.

K 2 rows to form foldline.
Change to 4½mm (US 7) needles.
**Next row** K3, (cast off 2 sts, K12 including st used to cast off) 7 times, cast off 2 sts, K to end.
**Next row** P to end, casting on 2 sts over those cast off in previous row.
Work 6 rows st st, beg with a K row.
Cast off loosely.
Fold front bands on to ws and catch down.
**Collar**
Using 5½mm (US 9) needles and chosen yarn, with rs of work facing, K up 66 sts evenly around neck edge.
Work 11 rows K1, P1 rib.
Cast off in rib.
Neaten buttonholes. Sew on buttons.

(Above and overleaf)
*This is another idea for using the step motif. Try it on any sleeveless V-neck shape (it will adapt to almost any number of stitches but choose a pattern worked intarsia). The Large Steps pattern is used on the back and an inverted Small Steps layout on the front. I chose the colours specially for this backdrop of weathered Maltese walls.*

Chart 2

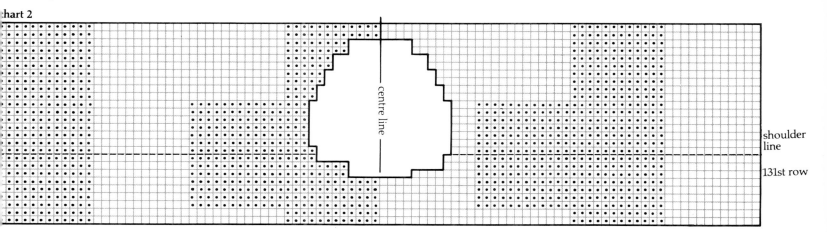

centre line

shoulder line

131st row

57

# Zigzag

This is a quick and easy two-colours-a-row design (though often I do 'cheat' and add a third colour just to break up the stripey effect). The structure is very simple, a vertical zigzag with a little decoration added to the points. You can arrange the colours so that you get the long up and down striped look (as on the chart), or by alternating light and dark it takes on a chequered look.

It's a superb vehicle for colour. If enough colour changes are introduced, you get a much more richly complex feeling than the two-colour form would seem to allow.

## V-neck Sweater

In this version there are about twenty colours in the darker stripes and seventeen lighter colours for contrast. The colouring came from a photograph of a room in Charleston, home of Bloomsburyite artist Duncan Grant. There was a gorgeous warm array of toasty ochres, pinks and grey-browns. The lavenders and cool silver greys add an important balancing note to the scheme, and there's a wide range of textures—mohair, wool, cotton chenille, silk and flecked tweeds.

MATERIALS
Approx 300[350,375]g (11[13,14]oz) mixed yarns
    averaging Aran/medium-weight in each of two
    groups of colours (A and B)
1 pair each 4½mm (US 7) and 5½mm (US 9)
    needles

TENSION
18 sts and 21 rows to 10cm (4in) over patt on
5½mm (US 9) needles.

MEASUREMENTS
**To fit bust/chest** 86[91,96]cm (34[36,38]in)
**Actual width** 91[96,100]cm (36[37½,40]in)
**Length to shoulder** 55[57,59]cm (21½[22½,23]in)
**Side seam** 32[33,34]cm (12½[13,13½]in)
**Sleeve seam** 45[47,48]cm (17½[18½,19]in)

BACK
Using 4½mm (US 7) needles and yarn A or B, cast on 68[72,76] sts.
Work 13 rows K1, P1 rib, in stripes at random.
**Next row** Rib 8[3,5], K up st between last st and next st to make 1, (rib 4[5,5], make 1) to last 8[4,6] sts, rib to end. 82[86,90] sts.
Change to 5½mm (US 9) needles and commence colour patt from chart on page 62, working in st st and weaving contrast colours into back of work, using one of the yarns from the A group and one from the B group as foll:
**1st row** (rs) K2 [4,6]B, (6A, 6B) to last 8[10,12] sts, 6A, 2[4,6]B.
**2nd row** P3B [5B,(1A, 6B)], (6A, 6B) to last 7[9,11] sts, 6A, 1[3,5]B.
Cont in patt as set, rep 1st–14th rows changing to different colours in groups A and B at random but working with only two colours to a row, until 106[110,114] rows have been worked in colour patt, thus ending with a P row.

**Shape shoulders**
Cast off 9[11,11] sts at beg of next 2 rows and 9[9,10] sts at beg of foll 4 rows.
Leave rem 28 sts on a spare needle.

FRONT
Work as given for back until 64[68,72] rows have been worked in colour patt, ending with a P row.
**Divide for neck**
**Next row** Patt 39[41,43] sts, K2 tog, K2 tog tbl, patt to end.
**Next row** Patt to neck edge, turn, leaving rem sts on a spare needle, cont on these sts only for right side of neck. 40[42,44] sts.
Work 1 row.
Keeping colour patt correct, dec 1 st at neck edge on next and every foll 3rd row until 27[29,31] sts rem, ending at armhole edge.
Work straight until front matches back to shoulder, ending at armhole edge.
**Shape shoulder**
Cast off 9[11,11] sts at beg of next row and 9[9,10] sts at beg of foll 2 alt rows.
With ws facing, rejoin yarn to sts on spare needle at neck edge, patt to end. Complete left side to match right side.

SLEEVES
Using 4½mm (US 7) needles and yarn A or B, cast on 34 sts.
Work 13 rows K1, P1 as for back.
**Next row** Rib 1, make 1 (rib 3, make 1) 11 times. 46 sts.
Change to 5½mm (US 9) needles and commence colour patt from chart, work in st st beg with a K row and working between sleeve markers, *at the same time* inc 1 st at each end of 3rd and every foll 4th row until there are 82[86,90] sts.
Now work straight until 84[88,90] rows in all have been worked in colour patt.
Cast off loosely.

TO MAKE UP
Backstitch left shoulder seam.
**Neckband**
Using 4½mm (US 7) needles and yarn A or B, with rs facing K across 28 sts left at back neck, then K up 47 sts down left side of neck and 46 sts up right side of neck. 121 sts.
Work in K1, P1 rib as foll:
**1st row** (ws) Rib 44, P2 tog, P2 tog tbl, rib to end. 119 sts.
**2nd row** Rib 72, K2 tog tbl, K2 tog, rib to end of row. 117 sts.
**3rd row** Rib 42, P2 tog, P2 tog tbl, rib to end of row. 115 sts.
Cont to dec at front neck in this way, working knitwise decs on rs of work and purlwise decs on ws, rib 6 more rows. 103 sts.
Cast off, working decs as before.
Backstitch right shoulder seam.
Set in sleeves flat, using a backstitch seam, matching centre of cast-off edge of sleeve to shoulder seam.
Backstitch side and sleeve seams.

*(Far right) I like the way the toasty colours of this V-neck sweater are underlined by the bronze foliage of young rose bushes.*

# Steps & Zigzags

## *Jacket*

I've done lots of colour schemes with this design. It takes anything from pale pearly colourings to rich dark tweeds. Alternatively, try the grey-blue colourway on page 64—a range of purply blues and dark greys for the 'silhouette', with shots of sunlit cream sand and water colours between. It was photographed in Malta and that special light and painted walls made it dance with life. This zigzag is very symmetrical but I often knit it with uneven numbers of rows between the turning points.

### MATERIALS
Approx 700g (25oz) mixed yarns averaging
   chunky weight in each of two groups of colours
   (A and B)
1 pair each 4½mm (US 7), 5½mm (US 9) and
   6½mm (US 10½) needles
8 buttons

### TENSION
16 sts and 18 rows to 10cm (4in) over patt on 6½mm (US 10½) needles.

### MEASUREMENTS
**To fit bust/chest** up to 111cm (44in)
**Actual width** 142cm (56in)
**Length to shoulder** 78cm (31in)
**Side seam** 51cm (20in)
**Sleeve seam** 41cm (16in)

### BACK AND FRONTS (one piece)
Using 5½mm (US 9) needles and yarn A or B, cast on 92 sts.
Work 13 rows K1, P1 rib, striped at random.
**Next row** Rib 4, K up st between last st and next st to make 1, (rib 4, make 1) to last 4 sts, rib 4. 114 sts.
Change to 6½mm (US 10½) needles and commence colour patt from chart, working in st st throughout, weaving contrast yarns into back of work and using one of the yarns from the A group and one from the B group as foll:

**1st row** (rs) K6B, (6A, 6B) 9 times.
**2nd row** P(1A, 6B, 5A) 9 times, 1A, 5B.
Cont in patt as set, rep 1st–14th rows changing to different colours in groups A and B at random but working with only two colours to a row, until 128 rows in all have been worked in zigzag part, thus ending with a P row (mark each end of 10th and 44th rows for pockets).
### Divide for fronts
**Next row** Patt 52 sts, cast off 10 sts, patt to end.
**Next row** Patt to next edge, turn, leaving rem sts on a spare needle, cont on these sts for left side. 52 sts.
### Shape neck
Cast off 4 sts at beg of next row (this row marks the shoulder line), then dec 1 st at beg of foll alt row. 47 sts.
Work 5 rows without shaping, thus ending at neck edge.
Cast on 1 st at beg of next and foll 2 alt rows, then 3 sts at beg of next alt row and 4 sts at beg of foll alt row. 57 sts.
Now work straight until left front is same length as back from shoulder line to top of rib, ending with a P row, and marking each end of equivalent rows on back for pockets.
Change to 5½mm (US 9) needles and yarn A or B.
**Next row** (K1, P1, K1, P2 tog) to last 2 sts, K1, P1. 46 sts.
Work 14 rows K1, P1 rib, in stripes as for back. Cast off in rib.
With ws facing, rejoin yarn to neck edge and complete right side to match left, reversing shapings.

### SLEEVES
Using 5½mm (US 9) needles and yarn A or B, cast on 34 sts.
Work 13 rows K1, P1 rib, in stripes at random.
**Next row** Rib 3, make 1, (rib 4, make 1) to last 3 sts, rib 3. 42 sts.
Change to 6½mm (US 10½) needles and commence colour patt from chart, work in st st beg with a K row, working between sleeve markers, *at the same time* inc 1 st at each end of 3rd

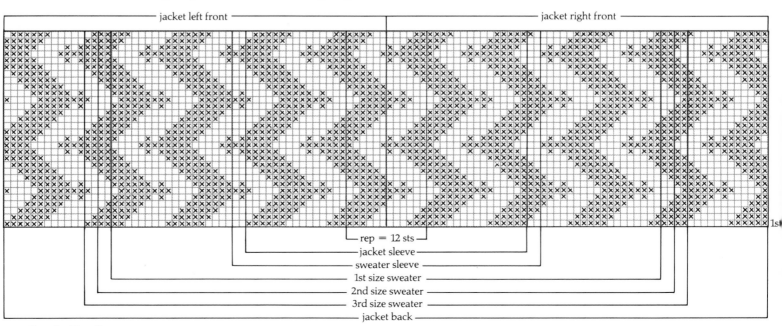

jacket left front — jacket right front

rep = 12 sts
jacket sleeve
sweater sleeve
1st size sweater
2nd size sweater
3rd size sweater
jacket back

**Key** □ = A  ☒ = B

and every foll alt row until there are 104 sts, ending with a P row (64 patt rows in all have been worked).
Cast off loosely.

## LEFT POCKET LINING
Using 6½mm (US 10½) needles and yarn A or B, with rs facing, K up 26 sts between pocket markers on left side back edge.
Work in st st beg with a P row, cast on 4 sts at beg of 1st row, then dec 1 st at beg of next and every foll K row until 17 sts rem.
Cast off.

## RIGHT POCKET LINING
Work as for left pocket lining, working between pocket markers on right back side edge, and reversing shapings.

## POCKET EDGINGS
Using 5½mm (US 9) needles and yarn A or B, with rs facing, K up 26 sts between pocket markers.
K 1 row to form foldline. Work 4 rows st st, beg with a K row.
Cast off loosely.

## BUTTON BAND
Using 5½mm (US 9) needles and yarn A or B, with rs facing, K up 115 sts (12 on rib, 103 sts on main part) along right front edge (for a man's jacket, left front edge for a woman's). P 1 row.
K 2 rows to form foldline. Change to 4½mm (US 7) needles and work 8 rows st st beg with a K row.
Cast off loosely.

## BUTTONHOLE BAND
Using 5½mm (US 9) needles and yarn A or B, with rs facing, K up 115 sts as given for button band along left front edge (for a man's jacket, right front edge for a woman's), *at the same time* make buttonholes on K up row as foll:
**K up and buttonhole row** K up 4 sts, (K up 2 sts, lift 2nd st on right-hand needle over 1st st and off needle, K up 1 st, lift 2nd st on right-hand needle over 1st st and off, K up 12) 8 times, ending last rep K up 3.
**Next row** P to end, casting on 2 sts over those cast off in previous row. 115 sts.
K 2 rows to form foldline.
Change to 4½mm (US 7) needles.
**Next row** K4, (cast off 2 sts, K13 including st used to cast off) to last 6 sts, cast off 2 sts, K to end.
**Next row** P to end, casting on 2 sts over those cast off in previous row.
Work 8 rows st st, beg with a K row.
Cast off loosely.

## TO MAKE UP
Set sleeves in flat, matching centre of cast-off edge of sleeve to shoulder line.
Fold pocket edges on to ws and catch down.
Backstitch side and sleeve seams. Catch down pocket linings to ws of fronts.
Fold button and buttonhole bands on to ws and catch down.
**Collar**
Using 5½mm (US 9) needles and yarn A or B,

with rs facing, K up 68 sts evenly around neck edge.
Work 14 rows K1, P1 rib, in stripes at random as for back.
Cast off in rib.
Neaten buttonholes.
Sew on buttons.

## Coat

There's almost a biblical effect to the colours in this coat. I used chunky tweeds, thick chenilles and big fuzzy bouclés, as well as mohair and wool. The colours are rich and fairly bright for the most part—magentas, purples, bottle green, deep rusty red and darkest aubergine. The light colours are mellow and medium bright—sky blue, pink and camel.

*(Overleaf) A typical tiled Maltese wall makes a sharp arrangement with the Zigzag Jacket. Try these zigzags on a Fair Isle slipover pattern and give it a striped ribbed neckband or, as here (inset), one in patterned stocking stitch. Or try them on a kimono coat (possibly the Dark Star Coat, page 96) to make something like the one below, which is photographed with the Tumbling Blocks Sweater (page 76).*

# DIAMONDS

From harlequins and crystals to sporty Argyll checks, diamonds are a classic motif that has been used in just about every kind of decorative art. They are immensely versatile. Diamonds can be elegant or bold and joyous (to me the shape always has a really happy feeling), and they also lend themselves to extremes of scale from sharp, sophisticated little borders to huge circus wagon decorations. Simple two-colour patterns on bark cloth, carved wood or woven grasses abound in the crafts of the Australian Aborigines, Pacific Islanders and American Indians. A much richer use of colour within the diamond format can be seen in Russian embroidery and carpets and, in a different mood, on Sicilian painted wagons.

Large jacket and coat shapes can be beautifully broken up by diamonds—the elongated type have a definite lengthening and slimming effect on the body. In the first two of my diamond patterns I've quartered the shape, which gives plenty of scope for exciting colour experiments.

When working out a colour scheme, I find that the ribs are often a stumbling block. You have to decide what colours they are going to be before the main part of the garment has been worked, and before you can really tell what will best enhance the design (you've probably noticed by now that my ribs are almost always striped). One way in which we sometimes get over this difficulty, especially when making jackets and coats, is to work the ribs, including those on the lower edges, last. You simply knit up the required number of stitches around the bottom after the side seams have been joined, and knit the rib downwards. This way, if you're designing for yourself, you can get the exact degree of 'blouson' that you want and, more importantly, you can base the colouring on what has happened in the garment.

The patterns in this book have all been written in the conventional way (that is, with the ribs worked first) and, if you're using exactly the same colours, the problem does not arise. However, if you are working out your own scheme and you want to try this method, simply begin your garment above the rib by casting on the number of stitches given at the end of the increase row. Later pick up the original number of cast-on stitches along the same edge for working the rib. Cast off the rib loosely (in rib), using larger needles if necessary, or the edge will be too tight and ungiving.

*(Far left) This ancient floor in Pompeii was the inspiration for the Jacket on page 79. The Diamond Tunic (inset and on page 72) is photographed against a wonderful lichen-encrusted wall. Of the many ways this tunic can be worn, I enjoy it particularly over this full cotton skirt.*

# Large Diamonds

These large diamonds always make me think of sails or kites. The idea of elongated diamonds was also appealing—I've always loved the look of this motif in Indian and Indonesian textiles and I was also thinking of that long spikiness in the pattern on backgammon boards.

## Jacket

The challenge here was to design a large jacket with a slimming line to the pattern. For the dark one (page 70) I began with sombre tones accented with royal blues and maroons, then I added a group of light silvers and dusty cool pinks and beiges. All these darks and the mixture of bouclés, chenilles, silks, wools and tweedy strands make for a luxurious, sumptuous garment. Gather two or three groups of yarns with as many shades, tones and textures in each one as you can manage (I used about sixty).

The red and blue colourway was invented for my cousin Heidi, who loves the softly bright colours of South America. I thought of water melons, flowery Peruvian and Mexican embroideries, and the turquoises of the Caribbean Sea. Most of the colours are clean and fresh, with the occasional dusty grey and a muted tweedy pink. I used some quite brilliant turquoises and pinks mixed with pearly greys or lavenders to tone them down. There aren't any really light brights, nor anything darker than a charcoal or deep magenta. Make all the colours within each point shade gently from tone to tone, while contrasting more strongly with the quarter-diamond next to it.

The sizing of this is rather generous, by the way, but it hangs beautifully and looks good on anyone, small or large.

(Right) *I love the way the magentas and scarlets of the red and blue colourway glow in a backlit patch of hollyhocks.*

(Overleaf) *This picture displays to full effect the magnificent width of the Large Diamond Jacket.*

MATERIALS
Approx 1500g (53oz) mixed yarns and colours averaging chunky weight
1 pair each 4½mm (US 7), 5½mm (US 9) and 6½mm (US 10½) needles
7 buttons

TENSION
13 sts and 19 rows to 10cm (4in) over st st on 6½mm (US 10½) needles.

MEASUREMENTS
**To fit bust/chest** 86cm–121cm (36–48in)
**Actual width** 184cm (74in)
**Length** 73cm (29in)
**Side seam** 47cm (18½in)
**Sleeve seam** 35cm (14in)

BACK, FRONTS AND SLEEVES (one piece)
Using 5½mm (US 9) needles and chosen yarn, cast on 90 sts.
Work 14 rows K1, P1 rib in stripes at random.
**Next row** Rib 2, K up loop between last st and next st to make 1, (rib 3, make 1) to last st, rib 1. 120 sts.
Change to 6½mm (US 10½) needles and commence colour patt from chart, working in st st and twisting yarns between colours to avoid holes (do not carry yarns across the back), use different groups of colours for each quarter-diamond, using up to 16 different colours as foll:
**1st row** (rs) K14A, 1B, 1C, 14D, 14E, 1F, 1G, 14H, 14J, 1L, 1M, 14N, 14Q, 1R, 1S, 14T.
**2nd row** P to end using same colours as in previous row.
Cont in patt as set changing colours as required, keeping the tones within each point close to each other but contrasting more strongly with adjacent points, work 76 rows from chart, marking each end of 9th and 43rd rows for pockets, ending with a ws row.
**Shape sleeves**
**77th row** Cast on 30 sts, patt across these sts then across body sts.
Using separate length of yarn cast on 30 sts on to free needle and cont 77th row across these sts also. 180 sts.
Cont in patt until 124 rows have been worked from chart, ending with a ws row.
**Divide for neck**
**Next row** Patt 86 sts, turn, leaving rem sts on a spare needle and cont on these sts only for right side of neck and right front. 86 sts.
Cast off 4 sts at beg of next row. 82 sts. (This point marks the shoulder line.)
Cont in patt, reversing diamonds as shown on chart *at the same time* cont to shape back neck as foll:
Work 1 row. Dec 1 st at beg of next row. 81 sts.
Work 7 rows straight, ending at neck edge.
**Shape front neck**
Cast on 1 st at beg of next and foll 2 alt rows, then 2 sts at beg of next alt row and 4 sts at beg of foll alt row. 90 sts.

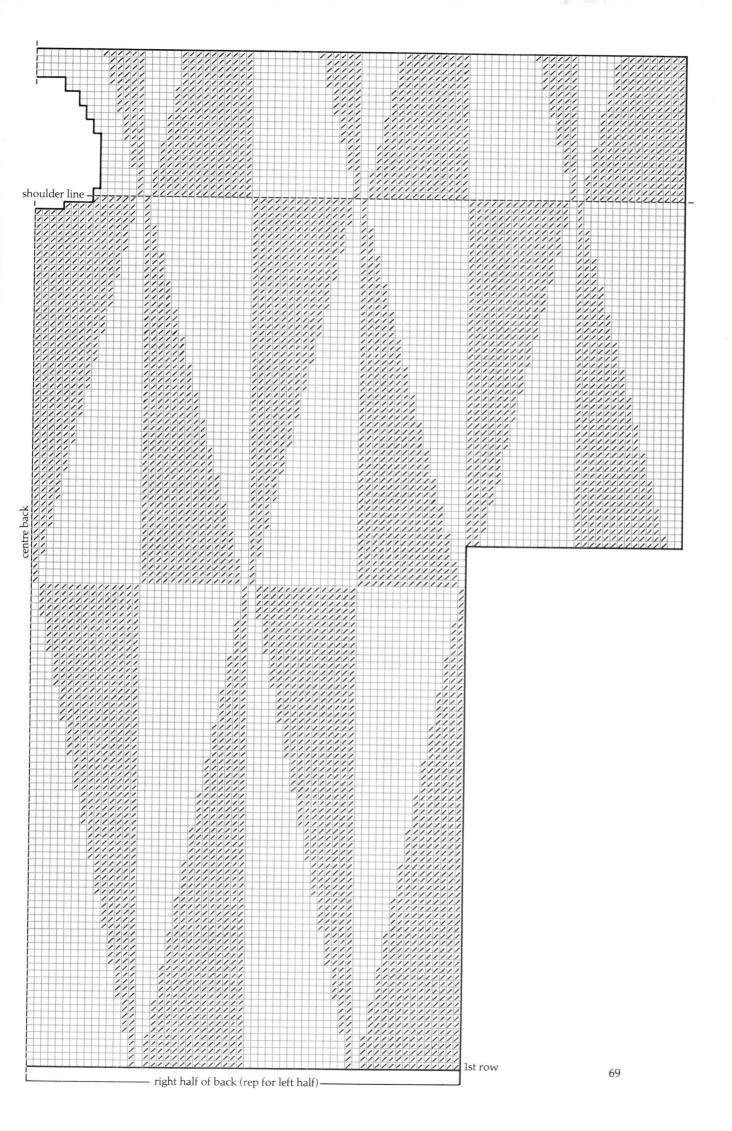

shoulder line

centre back

1st row

right half of back (rep for left half)

69

Diamonds

Now work straight until front sleeve matches
back sleeve from shoulder line (100 rows in all on
sleeve), ending at cuff edge.
**Next row** Cast off 30 sts, patt to end. 60 sts.
Now cont without shaping, reversing diamond
patt as before, until front matches back from
shoulder line to top of rib, ending with a P row
(mark equivalent rows on side edge front for
pocket).
Change to 5½mm (US 9) needles and yarn as for
back rib.
**Next row** (K1, P1, K2 tog, P1, K1, P2 tog) to last 4
sts, K1, P1, K2 tog. 45 sts.
Rib 14 rows in stripes at random.
Cast off in rib.
With rs facing, rejoin yarn to sts left on spare
needle at neck edge, cast off 8 sts, patt to end.
Work 1 row. (This point marks the shoulder line.)
Cast off 4 sts at beg of next row and 1 st at beg of
foll alt row. 81 sts.
Complete left front to match right, reversing
diamond patt from shoulder line and marking
equivalent rows on side edge for pocket.

POCKET LININGS AND EDGINGS
Work as given for Zigzag Jacket on page 63.

CUFFS
Using 5½mm (US 9) needles and chosen yarn,
with rs facing, K up 78 sts across sleeve end.
Work 5 rows st st, beg with a P row, in stripes at
random.
**Next row** (K2 tog) to end. 39 sts.
Work 5 rows st st stripes, beg with a P row.
**Next row** (K3, K2 tog) to last 4 sts, K4. 32 sts.
Work 14 rows K1, P1 rib.
Cast off in rib.

BUTTON BAND
Using 5½mm (US 9) needles and chosen yarn,
with rs facing, K up 102 sts (12 on rib, 90 on main
part) along right front edge (for men, left front
edge for women).
P 1 row.
K 2 rows to form foldline.
Change to 4½mm (US 7) needles and work 8
rows st st, beg with a K row.
Cast off loosely.

BUTTONHOLE BAND
Using 5½mm (US 9) needles and chosen yarn,
with rs facing, K up 102 sts as for button band
along remaining front edge, *at the same time* make
buttonholes on K up row as foll:
**K up and buttonhole row** K up 2 sts, (K up 2 sts,
lift 2nd st on right-hand needle over 1st st and off
needle, K up 1 st, lift 2nd st on right-hand needle
over 1st st and off, K up 13) 7 times, ending last
rep K up 1.
**Next row** P to end, casting on sts over those cast
off in previous row.
K 2 rows to form foldline.
Change to 4½mm (US 7) needles.
**Next row** K2, (cast off 2 sts, K14 including st used
to cast off) to last 4 sts, cast off 2 sts, K to end.
**Next row** P to end, casting on 2 sts over those cast
off in previous row.
Work 6 rows st st beg with a K row.
Cast off loosely.

TO MAKE UP
Fold pocket edgings on to ws and catch down.
Backstitch side and sleeve seams.
Catch down pocket linings on to ws of fronts.
Fold button and buttonhole bands on to ws and
catch down.
**Collar**
Using 5½mm (US 9) needles, with rs facing, K up
64 sts evenly round neck edge.
Work 14 rows K1, P1 rib in stripes at random.
Cast off in rib.
Neaten buttonholes. Sew on buttons.

# Tunic and Dress

The colours in the tunic were inspired by
Picasso's rose period paintings of harlequins.
Those faded, sundrenched, rather chalky colours
look wonderful on tanned skin. This particular
garment was made in raw silk and cotton. I
envisaged it being worn casually walking along a
beach or elegantly over a light cotton skirt in the
evening.
  The colours in the dress were invented to make
use of the colours of the stones in the English
Lake District—the blue-greens and mossy greens
were delicious to work with. I added pinks and
lavenders, mostly in silks and cottons, including
cotton chenilles. The design is large, so I played
down the dynamic scale of the diamonds by
using these quite close tones, but you could go
mad and do it in primrose and gunmetal or
something really sharp in contrast. The dress, by
the way, is the same as the tunic with one
diamond added to the length.

MATERIALS
**Dress** approx 975g (35oz) mixed yarns and
    colours averaging chunky weight
**Tunic** approx 725g (26oz)
1 pair each 4mm (US 6) and 5mm (US 8) needles
1 set four double-pointed 4mm (US 6) needles (or
    circular needle)

TENSION
18 sts and 24 rows to 10cm (4in) over patt on 5mm
(US 8) needles.

MEASUREMENTS
**To fit bust** up to 96cm (38in)
**Actual width** 100cm (40in)
**Dress length to shoulder** 105cm (41½in)
**Tunic length to shoulder** 70cm (27½in)
**Dress side seam** 76cm (30in)
**Tunic side seam** 41cm (16in)
**Sleeve seam** 8cm (3in)

BACK, FRONT AND SLEEVES (one piece)
Using 4mm (US 6) needles and chosen yarn, beg
at lower front edge, cast on 90 sts.
Work 8 rows st st beg with a K row. P 2 rows to
form hemline.
Change to 5mm (US 8) needles and commence
colour patt from chart, working in st st, twisting
yarns between colours to avoid holes, and using
a different colour or group of colours for each
quarter diamond, rep chart 3 times across rows.
Cont in patt until 98 chart rows have been worked
for tunic, or 182 rows for dress, end with ws row.

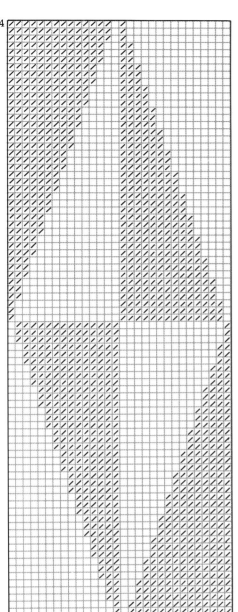

84

rep = 30 sts

1st row

**Shape sleeves**
Cast on 15 sts at beg of next 2 rows. 120 sts.
Work 60 rows straight.
**Divide for neck**
**Next row** Patt 48 sts, cast off 24 sts, patt to end.
**Next row** Patt to neck edge, turn, leaving rem sts on a spare needle and cont on these sts only for right side of neck. 48 sts.
** Dec 1 st at neck edge on next and every alt row until there are 45 sts.
Work straight until 168th patt row (for tunic) or 252nd patt row (for dress) has been completed. This point marks the shoulder line.
Work 2 rows.
Now inc 1 st at neck edge on next and foll 2 alt rows. **Cast on 24 sts at end of next row, leave these sts on a spare needle.
With ws facing, rejoin yarn to left neck edge and complete left side to match right side working from ** to **. 48 sts. Work 1 row.
Work next row across these 48 sts and across 72 sts on spare needle to join left and right sides.
Work 60 rows straight.
**Shape sleeves**
Cast off 15 sts at beg of next 2 rows. 90 sts.
Work 98 rows (for tunic) or 182 rows (for dress) without shaping.
Change to 4mm (US 6) needles.
K 2 rows to form hemline. Work 8 rows st st, beg with a K row. Cast off loosely.

TO MAKE UP
**Neck edging**
Using 4mm (US 6) double-pointed needles and chosen yarn, with rs facing K up 79 sts around neck edge. Work in rounds as foll: P 1 round for foldline, K 2 rounds. Cast off loosely.
**Armhole edgings**
Using 4mm (US 6) needles and chosen yarn, with rs facing, K up 103 sts around armhole edge.
K 1 row for foldline. Work 3 rows st st, beg with a K row. Cast off.
Fold edgings on to ws and catch down.
Join side seams.

(Left) *The milky blues, sky blues and turquoises in these faded walls play delightfully with those in the tunic. The light pouring into the room from the gaping ceiling created a soft almost luminous glow.*

(Overleaf) *Lengthened by one diamond, the tunic becomes a dress. Both are shown here amid the gorgeous amaryllis at the Keukenhof Gardens, near Amsterdam. This diamond pattern could also work very beautifully in a contrasting scheme like that of the Tumbling Blocks Crew-neck Sweater.*

# Tumbling Blocks

One of the most intriguing diamond patterns, Tumbling Blocks, can be seen in objects as various as patchwork quilts, floor tiles and marquetry boxes. A three-dimensional illusion can be created by using light tones on the same plane of each box, medium tones on another and dark tones on another (the chart opposite shows exactly what is meant by this).

If you ignore the light and shade effect, the design becomes another version of the classic harlequin diamonds, and this could look wonderful in bright colours with black, something reminiscent of the old Commedia dell'Arte costumes, perhaps. To enhance this impression, work a dark outline around each diamond (it would be easier to Swiss-darn this on afterwards—if you knit it in, carry the outline yarn across the back, but remember that this will tend to pull the fabric inwards, altering the tension and resulting in a narrower garment than the one shown here).

## Crew-neck Sweater

*The Tumbling Blocks pattern given two quite different treatments—a crew-neck sweater in deep pastels with black and charcoal and a jacket directly inspired by a floor in Pompeii (see page 66).*

The colouring for this came from those elegant patchwork quilts the Victorians used to make from outworn taffeta skirts and dressing gowns. The yarns used were mainly silks and wools. You can emphasize the patchwork effect by introducing a two-colour pattern into some of the diamond shapes (I love giving myself this 'impossible' sort of project).

MATERIALS
Approx 825g (29oz) mixed Aran/medium-weight yarns in each of three groups of colours—dark shades (A), medium shades (B) and light shades (C)
1 pair each 3¾mm (US 5) and 4½mm (US 7) needles

TENSION
19 sts and 24 rows to 10cm (4in) over patt on 4½mm (US 7) needles.

MEASUREMENTS
**To fit bust/chest** up to 102cm (up to 40in)
**Actual width** 105cm (41½in)
**Length to shoulder** 64cm (25½in)
**Side seam** 39cm (15½in)
**Sleeve seam** 55cm (21½in)

BACK
Using 3¾mm (US 5) needles and yarn A, cast on 86 sts.
Work 19 rows K1, P1 rib in stripes at random.
**Next row** Rib 4, K up loop between last st and next st to make 1, (rib 6, make 1) to last 4 sts, rib to end. 100 sts.
Change to 4½mm (US 7) needles and commence colour patt from chart, working in st st throughout, using separate lengths of yarn for each patch of colour and twisting yarns between colours to avoid holes (do not strand yarn across the back), as foll:

Tumbling Blocks

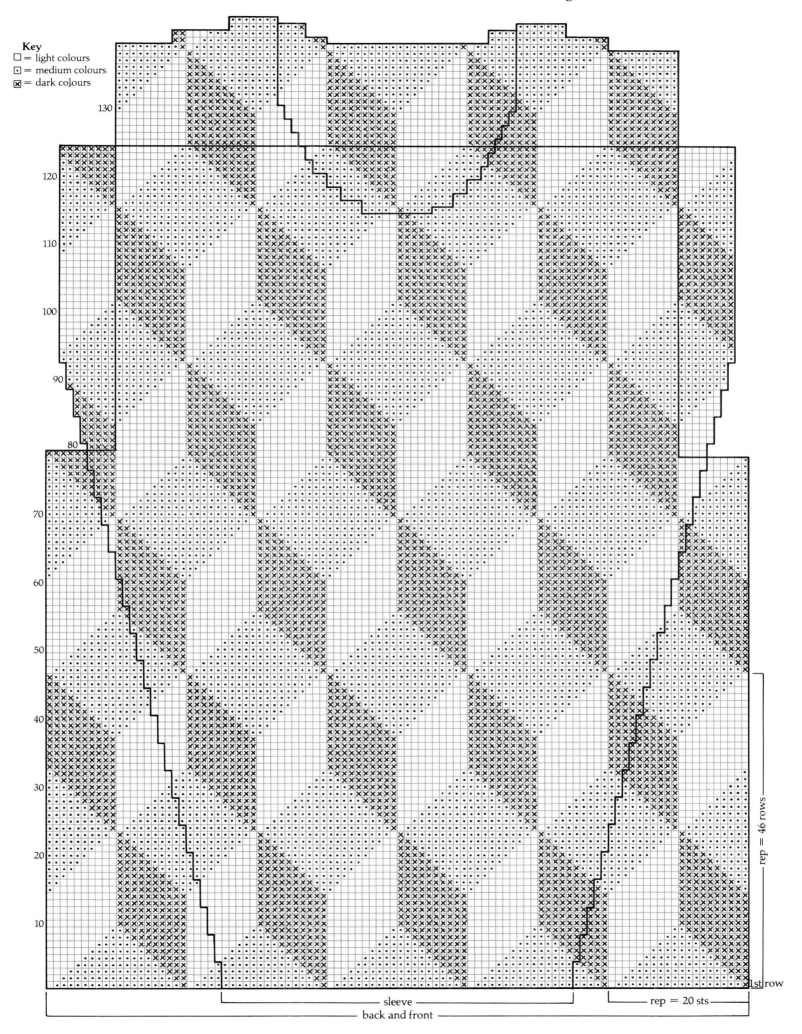

**Key**
□ = light colours
⊡ = medium colours
☒ = dark colours

130

120

110

100

90

80

70

60

50

40

30

20

10

sleeve

back and front

rep = 20 sts

rep = 46 rows

1st row

## Diamonds

**1st row** (rs) (K1A, 18B, 1C) 5 times.
**2nd row** (P2C, 16B, 2A) 5 times.
Cont in patt as set until 78 rows in all have been worked from chart, ending with a P row.
**Shape armholes**
Cast off 10 sts at beg of next 2 rows. 80 sts.
Cont in patt until 138 rows in all have been worked from chart.
**Shape shoulders and divide for neck**
**Next row** Cast off 8 sts, patt 24 sts including st used to cast off, cast off 16 sts, patt to end.
**Next row** Cast off 8 sts, patt to neck edge, turn, leaving rem sts on a spare needle, cont on these sts only for left side of back neck. 24 sts.
**Next row** Cast off 5 sts, patt to end. 19 sts.
**Next row** Cast off 8 sts, patt to end. 11 sts.
**Next row** Cast off 4 sts, patt to end.
Cast off rem 7 sts.
With ws of work facing, rejoin yarn to right side neck edge and complete to match left side, reversing shapings.

FRONT
Work as given for back until 114 rows have been worked from chart.
**Divide for neck**
**Next row** Patt 35 sts, cast off 10 sts, patt to end.
**Next row** Patt to end, turn, leaving rem sts on a spare needle and cont on these sts only for right side of neck.
Cast off 3 sts at neck edge on next row and 2 sts at beg of foll 2 alt rows. Now dec 1 st at neck edge on foll 5 alt rows. 23 sts.
Cont in patt without shaping until work matches back to shoulder, ending at armhole edge.

**Shape shoulder**
Cast off 8 sts at beg of next and foll alt row.
Work 1 row.
Cast off rem 7 sts.
With ws of work facing, rejoin yarn to left neck edge and complete to match right side, reversing shapings.

SLEEVES
Using 3¾mm (US 5) needles and yarn A, cast on 42 sts.
Work 19 rows K1, P1 rib in stripes at random.
**Next row** Rib 4, make 1, (rib 5, make 1) to last 3 sts, rib 3. 50 sts.
Change to 4½mm (US 7) needles and commence colour patt from chart working between sleeve markers, *at the same time* inc 1 st at each end of 5th and every foll 4th row until there are 96 sts.
Now work straight until 124 rows in all have been worked from chart.
Cast off loosely.

TO MAKE UP
Backstitch left shoulder seam.
**Neckband**
Using 3¾mm (US 5) needles and yarn A, with ws facing K up 40 sts across back neck and 68 sts evenly around front neck. 108 sts.
Work 8 rows K1, P1 rib in stripes at random.
Cast off in rib.
Backstitch right shoulder seam. Set in sleeves flat matching centre of cast-off edge of sleeve to shoulder line and joining last few rows of sleeve to cast-off sts at underarm.
Join side and sleeve seams.

*The Tumbling Blocks pattern creates several illusions depending on the arrangement of colours. In this quilt the pattern shifts dazzlingly from boxes to stars. You might borrow this approach for alternative versions of the jacket or sweater.*

# Pompeii Jacket

Steve's photograph of a tiled floor at Pompeii (page 66) was the direct inspiration for the jacket on page 80. Mohair plays an important part here to soften the colours and give them a lovely faded look. There's also wool, silk and cotton chenille—all creamy and muted tones with no stark whites or anything darker than medium grey.

## MATERIALS
Approx 1150g (41oz) mixed yarns and colours averaging chunky weight
1 pair each 4½mm (US 7), 5mm (US 8) and 6mm (US 10) needles
7 buttons

## TENSION
14 sts and 20 rows to 10cm (4in) over patt on 6mm (US 10) needles.

## MEASUREMENTS
**To fit bust/chest** up to 111cm (44in)
**Actual width** 143cm (56½in)
**Length to shoulder** 71cm (28in)
**Side seam** 44cm (17½in)
**Sleeve seam** 39cm (15½in) including cuff

## BACK
Using 5mm (US 8) needles and chosen yarn, cast on 80 sts. Work 14 rows K1, P1 rib.
**Next row** Rib 2, K up loop between last st and next st to make 1, (rib 4, make 1) to last 2 sts, rib 2. 100 sts.
Change to 6mm (US 10) needles and cont in st st beg with a K row, work 8 rows in stripes at random.
Now commence colour patt from chart on page 77 (do not foll chart for shaping), rep 1st–46th rows using a separate strand of yarn for each colour and twisting yarns between colours to avoid holes, work 68 rows straight, marking 10th and 43rd rows for pockets, ending with a ws row.
**Shape sleeves**
Cast on 40 sts at beg of next 2 rows. 180 sts. Cont in patt for 48 rows, ending with a ws row.
**Divide for neck and fronts**
**Next row** Patt 83 sts, turn, leaving rem sts on a spare needle and cont on these sts only for right side of neck.
Keeping patt correct, cast off 5 sts at neck edge on next row, then work 2 rows straight (this point marks the shoulder line). Now work 5 rows straight, ending at neck edge.
**Shape front neck**
Inc 1 st at neck edge on next and foll 2 alt rows. Work 1 row. Now cast on 3 sts at neck edge on next row and 6 sts on foll alt row. 90 sts.
Now work straight until front sleeve matches back sleeve from shoulder line, end at side edge.
**Shape front**
Cast off 40 sts at beg of next row. 50 sts.
Cont in patt until front matches back from shoulder line to beg of chart patt, marking equivalent rows on back for pockets, ending with a ws row. Work 8 rows in stripes as for back.
Change to 5mm (US 8) needles and yarn as for back rib and cont in K1, P1 rib as foll:

**Next row** (K1, P1, K2 tog, P1) to end. 40 sts.
Rib 14 rows. Cast off in rib.
With rs facing, rejoin yarn to neck edge.
**Next row** Cast off 14 sts, patt to end. 83 sts.
Work 1 row. Cast off 5 sts at neck edge on next row, then work 1 row straight (this point marks the shoulder line).
Now work 6 rows straight ending at neck edge. Complete left side to match right, marking equivalent rows on left front side edge for pockets.

## POCKET LININGS AND EDGINGS
Work as given for Zigzag Jacket on page 63. Using yarn as for back and front ribs, and 6mm (US 10) needles for linings and 5mm (US 8) needles for edgings.

## CUFFS
Using 6mm (US 10) needles and chosen yarn, with rs facing, K up 54 sts along sleeve edge. Work 5 rows st st in stripes at random.
**Next row** (K1, K2 tog) to end. 36 sts.
Change to 5mm (US 8) needles and yarn as for back and front ribs.
Work 14 rows K1, P1 rib. Cast off in rib.

## BUTTON BAND
Using 5mm (US 8) needles and yarn as for back and front ribs, with rs facing K up 100 sts (12 sts across rib and 88 across main part) along right front edge (for a man's jacket, left for a woman's). P 1 row. K 2 rows to form foldline.
Change to 4½mm (US 7) needles and work 8 rows st st beg with a K row. Cast off loosely.

## BUTTONHOLE BAND
Using 5mm (US 8) needles and yarn as for button band, with rs facing K up 100 sts as given for button band along left front edge (for a man's jacket and right front edge for a woman's), *at the same time* make buttonholes on K up row as foll:
**K up and buttonhole row** K up 4 sts, (K up 2 sts, lift 2nd st on right-hand needle over 1st st and off needle, K up 1 st, lift 2nd st on right-hand needle over 1st st and off, K up 12 sts) 7 times, ending last rep K up 3.
**Next row** P to end casting on 2 sts over those cast off in previous row.
K 2 rows to form foldline.
Change to 4½mm (US 7) needles.
**Next row** K4, (cast off 2 sts, K13 including st used to cast off) 6 times, cast off 2 sts, K to end.
**Next row** P to end casting on 2 sts over those cast off in previous row.
Work 6 rows st st, beg with a K row.
Cast off loosely.

## TO MAKE UP
Fold pocket edgings on to ws and catch down. Backstitch side and sleeve seams. Catch down pocket lining on to ws of jacket fronts. Fold button and buttonhole bands on to ws and catch down.
**Collar**
Using 5mm (US 8) needles and yarn as for button band, with rs facing K up 80 sts evenly around neck. Work 13 rows K1, P1 rib. Cast off in rib. Neaten buttonholes. Sew on buttons.

(Overleaf) *The Pompeii Jacket photographed with the Ribbon V-neck Sweater (page 110) against two huge bouquets of glorious Dutch blossoms in the Keukenhof Gardens near Amsterdam.*

# STARS

Stars occur frequently in nature (from starfish to galaxies), so it's not surprising that they have always been one of man's most potent symbols. On the whole they convey optimism and hope, but there is also a mysterious, almost magical and other-worldly feeling about them. They feature strongly in the endlessly inventive geometric compositions of Islamic art and decoration which have been among my greatest influences. The tiles, carved wood and stonework, embroideries and the wonderful illuminated scripts all deal with stars in delightful ways.

The patterns show only two types of star: the Circus Star, floating on a rich background, has a glowing, almost flower-like feeling; the Outlined Star has a more solid sculptural quality. There are many other types of star that one could use. I once made a jacket with a star composed of two super-imposed squares (see below). You can also make a six-pointed star from two equilateral triangles, one reversed on top of the other. Try working it out on graph paper and see the impression you get from placing them close together or wide apart. When the points touch interesting shapes appear between the stars and there's a marvellous all-over lattice effect. Working with strong shapes like these, you can be much more adventurous with your colourings without losing the overall structure of the pattern. I often like to use close tones that don't quite disappear into each other, which is difficult but well worth the effort when it works out successfully.

If you're stuck for colour ideas, buy a postcard reproduction of your favourite painting and use colours from that (Monet's 'Water Lilies', for example, would make a marvellous scheme). It's important to work hard at finding colours that are quite close to the original. This is not quite as easy as it sounds. I've noticed in my workshops that, when they're working from close-toned material, people often pick colours that are too dark or too light, so that the contrasts are too harsh. If the exact tones are hard to find, combine two thinner strands (for example, pink and blue to create a lavender).

Using an actual physical reference in this way is especially useful if you're making a garment for someone else. A picture (or a decorated china pot or a rug or scrap of fabric) is worth a thousand words when it comes to describing colours.

(Far left) *As well as some of my star garments you can see a marvellously varied collection of source material for star patterns. There are two old oriental carpets, a cotton crocheted cap from Morocco, and a Chinese Chequers board. The yellow, black, cream and turquoise needlepoint is a detail of a cushion kit I designed for Ehrman.*

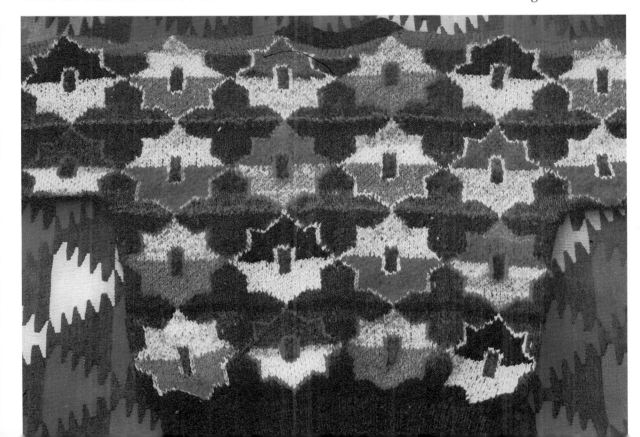

(Left) *This is the back of the jacket with the superimposed squares star motif. In this one the pattern is worked by the intarsia method, all the stars being different colours. It's lying on the kilim which was the inspiration for the Carpet Pattern (pages 40–45).*

Stars

# Circus Star

There was an oriental inspiration for this design, but it's also a homage to that great genius of colour, Matisse. With its bright, paper cut-out colours it reminds me of oriental circus costumes and, at the same time, of the famous Matisse collages. There are two versions of this design, one for children, the other, large and roomy, for an adult. The child's version has two colourways: the bright royal blue (specified in the pattern) and the deep dusky red both generate a marvellous feeling of carnival or celebration wherever they are worn.

MATERIALS
**Yarn used**
**Child's size** 225g (8oz) Rowan Yarns Double Knitting Wool in bright blue 57 (A); 25g (1oz) each in mid blue 50 (B), deep pink 96 (C), turquoise 90 (D), kingfisher 125 (E), bright pink 95 (F), deep red 67 (G), nile green 416 (H), dark olive 405 (J) and mauve 92 (L)
**Adult's size** 475g (17oz) in A; 75g (3oz) in G; 50g (2oz) each in C, D, E and F; 25g (1oz) each in B, H, J and L
**Equivalent yarn** double knitting
1 pair each 3¼mm (US 3) and 4mm (US 6) needles
1 set each four double-pointed 3¼mm (US 3) and 4mm (US 6) needles (or circular needles)

TENSION
25 sts and 26 rows to 10cm (4in) over patt on 4mm (US 6) needles.

## Child's Pullover

MEASUREMENTS
**To fit chest** 71cm (28in)
**Actual width** 78cm (31in)
**Length to shoulder** 53cm (21in)
**Side seam** 34cm (14in)
**Sleeve seam** 30cm (12in)

BACK, FRONT AND SLEEVES (one piece)
Beg at lower front edge, using 3¼mm (US 3) needles and yarn B, cast on 97 sts.
Work in K1, P1 rib as foll: 4 rows in C, 4 rows in D, 4 rows in E, 4 rows in F.
Change to 4mm (US 6) needles and yarn G. Work 2 rows st st, beg with a K row.

**Next row** K3G, (1A, 9G) to last 4 sts, 1A, 3G.
**Next row** P2G, (3A, 7G) to last 5 sts, 3A, 2G.
**Next row** K1G, (5A, 5G) to last 6 sts, 5A, 1G.
**Next row** P (7A, 3G) to last 7 sts, 7A.
**Next row** K8A, (1G, 9A) to last 9 sts, 1G, 8A.
With A, work 3 rows st st beg with a P row.
Cont in st st working star patt from chart, weaving in contrast colours across the back, as foll:
**1st row** (rs) *K6A, 1B, 3A, 1B, 5A; rep from * to last st, K1A.
**2nd row** P1A, *5A, 2B, 1A, 2B, 6A; rep from * to end of row.
Cont in patt as set, rep 1st–28th chart rows foll colour sequence table for contrast colours, until 68 rows in all have been worked in star patt, ending with a P row.
**Shape sleeves**
Keeping patt correct, cast on 45 sts at beg of next 2 rows. 187 sts.
**Next row** *K11A, 1D, 3A, 1D; rep from * to last 11 sts, 11A.
Cont in star patt as set work 22 rows, ending with a 9th patt row.
**Divide for neck**
**Next row** Patt 87 sts, turn, leaving rem sts on a spare needle, cont on these sts only for right side of neck and right sleeve.
**Shape front neck**
**Dec 1 st at neck edge on next 11 rows, and then on the 3 foll alt rows. 73 sts.
Work 9 rows without shaping, ending at neck edge.
**Shape back neck**
Cast on 5 sts at beg of next row and 6 sts at beg of foll alt row.** Work 1 row, leave these sts on a spare needle.
Return to sts on first spare needle. Sl centre 13 sts on a stitch holder; rejoin yarn to next st and patt to end.
Patt 1 row. Work as given for right side and sleeve from ** to **.
**Next row** Patt 84 sts, cast on 19 sts, patt 84 sts from spare needle. 187 sts.
**Next row** Patt to end across all sts.
Complete back reversing star patt, sleeve shaping, colour patt above rib and rib colours to make a mirror image of front.
Cast off in rib in B.

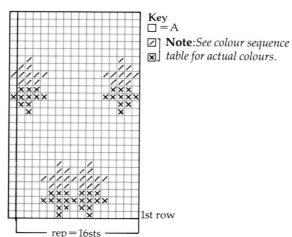

(Opposite) *Here is the dusky red Circus Star Pullover. The blue colourway behind is the one given in the patterns and can be seen more clearly in the adult version (page 87).*

Key
□ = A
☑ ⎤ **Note:** *See colour sequence*
☒ ⎦ *table for actual colours.*

1st row
— rep = 16sts —

COLOUR SEQUENCE TABLE
Use contrast colours for each band of stars as foll:

| band | ☒ | ☑ | band | ☒ | ☑ |
|------|---|---|------|---|---|
| 1 | B | F | 10 | B | J |
| 2 | H | D | 11 | E | F |
| 3 | J | L | 12 | G | D |
| 4 | C | B | 13 | L | E |
| 5 | E | L | 14 | B | C |
| 6 | D | G | 15 | L | J |
| 7 | F | E | 16 | D | H |
| 8 | J | B | 17 | F | B |
| 9 | D | C | | | |

Stars

NECKBAND
Using double-pointed 4mm (US 6) needles and yarn A, with rs facing K up 108 sts around neck edge. K 1 round.
**Next round** (K5A, 1G) to end.
**Next round** (K1G, 3A, 2G) to end.
**Next round** (K2G, 1A, 3G) to end.
Change to double-pointed 3¼mm (US 3) needles and work in K1, P1 rib as foll: 2 rounds in F, 2 rounds in E, 2 rounds in D, 2 rounds in C.
Cast off loosely in rib in B.

CUFF
Using 4mm (US 6) needles and yarn A, with rs facing K up 65 sts along sleeve edge.
Work 3 rows st st, beg with a P row, dec 1 st at each end of 2nd row. 63 sts.
**Next row** K2G tog, (9A, 1G) to end, ending last rep K2G tog. 61 sts.
**Next row** P2G, (7A, 3G) to end, ending last rep P2G instead of 3G.
**Next row** K2G tog, 1G, (5A, 5G) to end, ending last rep 1G, K2G tog. 59 sts.
**Next row** P3G, (3A, 7G) to end, ending last rep 3G instead of 7G.
**Next row** K2G tog, 2G, (1A, 9G) to end, ending last rep 2G, K2G tog. 57 sts.
**Next row** P3G, (1A, 9G) to end, ending last rep 3G instead of 9G.
Cont in st st, keeping (1A, 9G), panels correct dec 1 st at each end of next and every alt row until 47 sts rem, ending with a P row.
**Next row** K to end in G.
Change to 3¼mm (US 3) needles and work in K1, P1 rib as foll: 4 rows in F, 4 rows in E, 4 rows in D, 4 rows in C.
Cast off in B.

TO MAKE UP
Join side and sleeve seams.

## Adult's Pullover

MEASUREMENTS
**To fit bust** up to 107cm (42in)
**Actual width** 116cm (45½in)
**Length to shoulder** 73cm (29in)
**Side seam** 45cm (17½in)
**Sleeve seam** 40cm (16in)

BACK, FRONT AND SLEEVES (one piece)
Beg at lower front edge, using 3¼mm (US 3) needles and yarn B, cast on 131 sts.
Work 16 rows K1, P1 rib as for child's version.
**Next row** With F, rib 7, (K up loop between last st and next st to make 1, rib 9) 13 times, make 1, rib to end. 145 sts.
Change to 4mm (US 6) needles and yarn G.
Work 2 rows st st, beg with a K row.
**Next row** K2G, (1A, 9G) to last 3 sts, 1A, 2G.
**Next row** P1G, (3A, 7G) to last 4 sts, 3A, 1G.
**Next row** (K5A, 5G) to last 5 sts, 5A.
**Next row** P6A, 3G, (7A, 3G) to last 6 sts, 6A
**Next row** K7A, (1G, 9A) to last 8 sts, 1G, 7A.
With A, work 3 rows st st, beg with a P row.
Cont in st st working star patt from chart as given for child's version but work 96 rows before sleeve shaping instead of 68 and foll the colour sequence table on the right.

**Shape sleeves**
Keeping patt correct, cast on 10 sts at beg of next 14 rows. 285 sts.
Work straight until 138 rows in all have been worked in star patt from chart, thus ending with a ws row.
**Divide for neck**
**Next row** Patt 132 sts, turn, leaving rem sts on a spare needle and cont on these sts only for left side of neck and sleeve.
**Shape front neck**
**Dec 1 st at neck edge on next 8 rows, and then on foll 7 alt rows. 117 sts.
Work 14 rows without shaping ending at neck edge.
**Shape back neck**
Cast on 5 sts at beg of next and foll alt row. 127 sts. *Work 1 row, leave these sts on a spare needle.
Return to sts on first spare needle. Sl centre 21 sts on a st holder, with rs facing rejoin yarn to next st and patt to end.
Patt 1 row.
Work as given for left side from ** to *.
**Next row** Patt 127 sts, cast on 31 sts, patt 127 sts from spare needle. 285 sts.
**Next row** Patt to end across all sts.
Complete back as given for child's version working a dec row at top of rib as foll:
**Decrease row** With F, K2 tog, (rib 9, K2 tog) to end. 131 sts.

NECKBAND
Using double-pointed 4mm (US 6) needles and yarn A, with rs facing K up 150 sts evenly round neck edge (including 21 sts from st holder at centre front).
K 2 rounds.
**Next round** (K9A, 1G) to end.
**Next round** (K1G, 7A, 2G) to end.
**Next round** (K2G, 5A, 3G) to end.
**Next round** (K3G, 3A, 4G) to end.
**Next round** (K4G, 1A, 5G) to end.
**Next round** K to end in G.
Change to double-pointed 3¼mm (US 3) needles.
**Next round** With F, *(K1, P1) 3 times, K1, P2 tog; rep from * to last 6 sts, (K1, P1) 3 times. 134 sts.
Now work in K1, P1 rib as foll: 1 round in F, 2 rounds in E, 2 rounds in D, 2 rounds in C and 1 round in B.
Cast off in rib in B.

COLOUR SEQUENCE TABLE
Use contrast colours for each band of stars as foll:

| band | ☒ | ☑ |
|------|------|------|
| 1–9 | as child's version | |
| 10 | F | H |
| 11 | E | G |
| 12 | J | C |
| 13 | L | H |
| 14 | C | J |
| 15 | G | E |
| 16 | H | F |
| 17 | C | D |
| 18–26 | as bands 10–17 of child's version | |

CUFFS

Using 4mm (US 6) needles and yarn A, with rs facing K up 103 sts from edge of sleeve.
Work 3 rows st st, beg with a P row, dec 1 st each end of 2nd row. 101 sts.
**Next row** (rs) K2 tog A, 8A, (1G, 9A) to end, ending last rep, 8A, K2A tog. 99 sts.
**Next row** (P1G, 7A, 2G) to end, end last rep 1G.
**Next row** K2G tog, (5A, 5G) to end, end last rep 5A, K2G tog. 97 sts.
**Next row** (P2G, 3A, 5G) to end, end last rep 2G.

**Next row** K2G tog, 1G, (1A, 9G) to end, ending last rep 1G, K2G tog. 95 sts.
Cont in st st, keeping (1A, 9G) panels correct dec 1 st each end of next and every alt row until 85 sts rem.
**Next row** With G, P1, (P2 tog, P2) to end. 64 sts.
Change to 3¼mm (US 3) needles and complete as given for child's version.

TO MAKE UP
Join side and sleeve seams.

*These pure deep pastels create a joyous glow of colour. The Star Waistcoat (page 100) is in the background.*

# Outlined Star

This is a three-colours-a-row design. There's a background colour which changes about half way up each star, a star colour which changes at the same time as the background colour, and an outline colour which changes on some garments but on others the same colour is used for each row of stars.

The basic eight-pointed star shape is the same for each pattern, but there are slight differences in the way it is charted. The points of the stars are touching in some of the designs; in others there is one stitch in the background colour between each one. The scale of the star also changes from the small, jewel-like pattern of the children's crew-neck sweaters to the drama of the coat (page 96).

## Child's Crew-neck Sweater

These lovely little chunky sweaters are rich in detail and also as warm as toast with their three-colours-a-row thickness. Being child-sized, they are good patterns to begin with; you can get used to the design before tackling anything larger. You can make it in one of the colourways illustrated on page 90 (the pastels version is the one specified in the pattern), though it would look equally good in dozens of different schemes—you could go to town on bright colours or try something very subtle and tweedy, like the sleeveless pullover on page 97.

MATERIALS
**Yarn used**
50g (2oz) Rowan Yarns Double Knitting Wool
  each in silver grey 120 (A), silver blue 64 (D)
  and peach 79 (N); 25g (1oz) each in blue 51 (B),
  light turquoise 89 (C), acid green 32 (E), pale
  yellow 30 (F), sky blue 123 (G), silver 58 (H),
  lavender 121 (J), mauve 92 (L), pale pink 109
  (Q), lime green 76 (R)
50g (2oz) Rowan Yarns Light Tweed each in
  lavender 213 (S), grey 209 (T), scoured 201 (U)
  and silver 208 (V) (all used double throughout)
**Equivalent yarn** double knitting
1 pair each 3¾mm (US 5) and 4½mm (US 7)
  needles
1 set each four double-pointed 3¾mm (US 5) and
  4½mm (US 7) needles (or circular needles)

TENSION
24 sts and 24 rows to 10cm (4in) over patt on
4½mm (US 7) needles.

MEASUREMENTS
**To fit chest** 71–76cm (28–30in)
**Actual width** 84cm (33in)
**Length to shoulder** 46cm (18½in)
**Side seam** 28cm (11in)
**Sleeve seam** 31cm (12in)

BACK, FRONT AND SLEEVES (one piece)
Beg at lower back edge, using 3¾mm (US 5)
needles and yarn B, cast on 88 sts. Work in K1, P1
rib as foll: 1 row B, 1 row C, 10 rows A.

**Next row** With A, rib 8, K up loop between next
st and last st to make 1, (rib 6, make 1) to last 8
sts, rib to end. 101 sts.
P 1 row in A.
Change to 4½mm (US 7) needles and commence
colour patt from chart, working in st st
throughout and weaving contrast yarns in on
back of work (on rows like 6th row, where no
background colour is used, carry background
colour along row in the usual way to ensure even
fabric), as foll:
**1st row** (rs) K1D, (4D, 1E, 9D, 1E, 5D) 5 times.
**2nd row** P(5D, 2E, 7D, 2E, 4D) 5 times, 1D.
Cont in patt as set, changing the background and
contrast colours as shown in colour sequence
table, until 60 rows in all have been worked from
chart.
**Shape sleeves**
Keeping chart patt correct, cast on 40 sts at beg of
next 2 rows. 181 sts.
Cont in patt until 98 rows in all have been worked
from chart.
**Divide for back neck**
**Next row** Patt 76 sts, turn, leaving rem sts on a
spare needle and cont on these sts only for right
side of neck.
*Cast off 5 sts at beg of next row and 4 sts at beg
of foll alt row. 67 sts.*
Work 3 rows straight.
(When half-way point is reached cont reading
chart rows in reverse order.)
**Shape front neck**
**Cast on 1 st at beg of next and foll alt row, 2 sts
at beg of next alt row, and 3 sts at beg of foll 2 alt
rows. 77 sts.**
Leave these sts on a spare needle.
Rejoin yarn to sts at centre back, cast off 29 sts,
patt to end. 76 sts. Work 1 row.
Complete left side of neck to match right side
from * to *, reading chart rows in reverse order as
before. Work 1 row.
**Shape front neck**
Complete to match first side from ** to **.
**91st row** Patt to end of row, turn and cast on 27

These chalky pastels heightened by a deep singing blue are soft without being insipid. Being all in one piece, this is an easy pattern to knit and ideal for experimenting with colour schemes on the Outlined Star design. The dark colourway (overleaf) uses Tibetan carpet colours, similar to those in the Star Waistcoat on page 100.

sts, cut off yarn, sl sts left on spare needle on to needle to rejoin fronts and complete neck. 181 sts. Cont in patt, work 28 rows without shaping across all sts.

**Shape sleeves**
Cast off 40 sts at beg of next 2 rows. 101 sts. Cont in patt, work 60 rows straight to complete chart,

thus ending with a P row.
Change to 3¾mm (US 5) needles. K 1 row in A.
**Next row** With A, P7, P2 tog, (P5, P2 tog) to last 8 sts, P to end. 88 sts.
Work in K1, P1 rib as foll: 10 rows in A, 1 row in C, 1 row in B.
Cast off in rib in B.

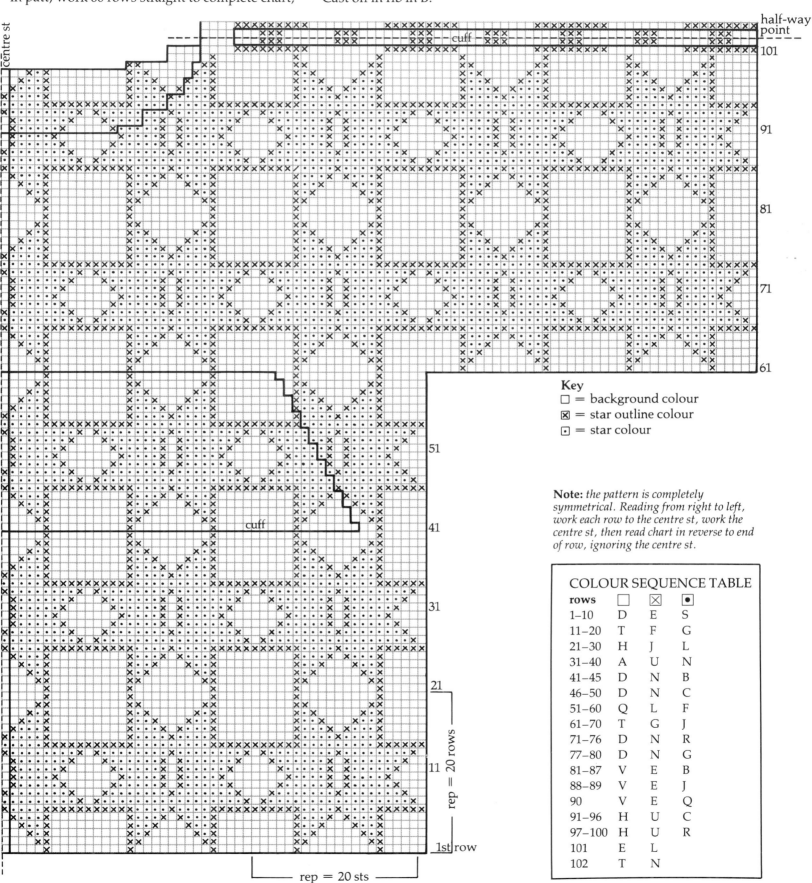

**Key**
□ = background colour
⊠ = star outline colour
⊡ = star colour

**Note:** *the pattern is completely symmetrical. Reading from right to left, work each row to the centre st, work the centre st, then read chart in reverse to end of row, ignoring the centre st.*

| COLOUR SEQUENCE TABLE | | | |
|---|---|---|---|
| **rows** | □ | ⊠ | ⊡ |
| 1–10 | D | E | S |
| 11–20 | T | F | G |
| 21–30 | H | J | L |
| 31–40 | A | U | N |
| 41–45 | D | N | B |
| 46–50 | D | N | C |
| 51–60 | Q | L | F |
| 61–70 | T | G | J |
| 71–76 | D | N | R |
| 77–80 | D | N | G |
| 81–87 | V | E | B |
| 88–89 | V | E | J |
| 90 | V | E | Q |
| 91–96 | H | U | C |
| 97–100 | H | U | R |
| 101 | E | L | |
| 102 | T | N | |

89

## Stars

### CUFFS
Using 4½mm (US 7) needles and yarn B, with rs facing K up 85 sts along sleeve end.
Commence colour patt from chart, beg with a P row, foll outline for cuff and beg at 41st row, *at the same time* dec 1 st at each end of 42nd chart row and every foll alt row until 65 sts rem.
Cont to dec as set, P 1 row in E, then work 102nd–103rd rows on chart between cuff markers, K 1 row in E. 61 sts.
Change to 3¾mm (US 5) needles and yarn A. Work in K1, P1 rib as foll:
**Next row** (Rib 4, K2 tog, P2 tog) to last 5 sts, rib 2, K2 tog, P1. 46 sts.
Rib 10 rows in A, 1 row in C, 1 row in B.
Cast off in rib in B.

### NECKBAND
Using double-pointed 4½mm (US 7) needles and yarn L, with rs facing K up 108 sts evenly around neck edge, beg at centre back.
**1st–2nd rounds** K(6T, 3N) to end.
K 1 round in L.
Change to 3¾mm (US 5) needles and work in K1, P1 rib as foll: 6 rows in A, 1 row in C, 1 row in B.
Cast off in rib in B.

### TO MAKE UP
Join side seams.

*I wanted to make a longer version of my basic Star Jacket pattern so I simply scaled the star motif up by a couple of stitches. This automatically makes the jacket longer and wider although you have the same number of stars in the body (but only two on the sleeves). By making simple adjustments in this way you can adapt many of the designs in this book to suit yourselves. Alternatively, try this colouring on the pattern for the yellow version.*

## Jacket

The jackets use slightly different versions of the same basic star pattern. Since they are knitted in chunky yarns rather than double knitting, this also means that the scale of the star is enlarged, though the principle of the design remains the same. The pattern is given for the yellow jacket which has a slightly smaller star than the grey version (below left).

I was introduced to the glories of yellow by the Peking Opera on a visit to London. Most of the costumes and sets on one scene were in shades of yellow. The impact of the sulphur yellow silk robes against a huge chrome yellow embroidered dragon was absolutely stunning!

When I proposed the idea of a star jacket in yellows (page 94), Steve suggested the shaded greys to fill them in, and the high pastels came from the china pots I've loved for years.

If you want to try this colouring, get at least ten shades (and textures, if possible) of yellow yarn—I used mohair, wool, chenille and a little silk. Then get a range of silver greys from dark to light (run lightest greys with cream or white to achieve the highest lights). Finally, collect the cleanest high pastels you can find (sky blues, pale turquoise, lavenders and pinks) and start knitting.

The grey jacket (left) suggests the colouring of some Japanese prints: the pale silver grey of the ground, with its flecks of light cream, and the pastels and deeper maroons and blues, like fragments of robes passing through a winter landscape. The contrasting outline is like a coloured light surrounding the stars. I often use quite arbitrary breaks of colour in this strong geometric pattern. But here, though contrasting, the colours are inherently soft, so the overall impression is gentle and almost silky (I used some raw silk, mohair and synthetic flecked yarns in with plain wool).

### MATERIALS
Approx 600g (22oz) mixed chunky yarns in a range of colours for the background (A), 200g (8oz) for star outline (B), and 400g (15oz) for star centres (C)
1 pair each 5½mm (US 9) and 6½mm (US 10½) needles
7 buttons

### TENSION
16 sts and 16½ rows to 10cm (4in) over patt on 6½mm (US 10½) needles.

### MEASUREMENTS
**To fit bust/chest** up to 101cm (40in)
**Actual width** 111cm (43½in)
**Length to shoulder** 80cm (31½in)
**Side seam** 51cm (20in)
**Sleeve seam** 48cm (20in) including cuff

### BACK, FRONTS AND SLEEVES (one piece)
Beg at lower back edge, using 5½mm (US 9) needles and yarn C, cast on 72 sts.
Change to yarn A.
Work 13 rows K1, P1 rib.
**Next row** Rib 6, K up loop between next st and

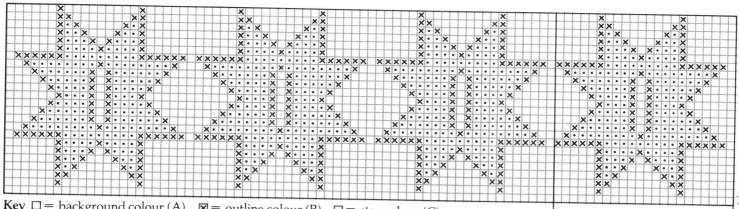

**Key** □ = background colour (A)  ⊠ = outline colour (B)  ⊡ = star colour (C)

1st row

rep = 22 sts

last st to make 1, (rib 4, make 1) to last 6 sts, rib 1, make 1, rib 5. 89 sts.
Change to 6½mm (US 10½) needles and commence colour patt from chart. Work in st st, weaving contrast colours into back of work, carrying all three colours to end of each row (on rows like 25th row, where no contrast colours are used, carry these across the back weaving them in as usual to maintain an even texture) as foll:
**1st row** With A, K to end.
**2nd row** P1A, (5A, 1B, 9A, 1B, 6A) 4 times.
**3rd row** K(6A, 2B, 7A, 2B, 5A) 4 times, 1A.
Cont in patt as set, changing colours as required but working with no more than 3 colours to a row, rep 1st–24th rows until 72 rows in all have been worked in star patt, thus ending with a P row (mark each end of 16th and 48th rows for pockets).
**Shape sleeves**
**Next row** Cast on 66 sts, patt across these and body sts, as given for 1st row but work rep 7 times instead of 4. 155 sts.
Now cast on 66 sts on to free needle and cont 1st row across these sts, working 3 more patt reps. 221 sts.
**Next row** Patt to end as given for 2nd row, working rep 10 times instead of 4.
Now work straight until 46 rows have been worked from beg of sleeve shaping, ending with a P row.
**Divide for fronts**
**Next row** Patt 105 sts, cast off 11 sts, patt to end.
**Next row** Patt to neck edge, turn, leaving rem sts on a spare needle for right front, cont on these sts only for left front. 105 sts.
Cast off 4 sts at beg of next row, then dec 1 st at beg of foll alt row. 100 sts.
Work 7 rows straight, ending at neck edge.
**Shape front neck**
Cast on 1 st at beg of next and foll 3 alt rows, then 2 sts at beg of next alt row, and 5 sts at beg of foll alt row. 111 sts.
Now work straight until 96 rows in all have been worked on sleeves (4 complete stars), ending with a P row.
Work 1 row, thus ending at sleeve edge.
**Next row** Cast off 66 sts, patt to end. 45 sts.
Now work straight until front matches back to top of rib, ending with a P row (mark equivalent rows on front for pockets).
Change to 5½mm (US 9) needles and yarn A.
**Next row** (K1, P2 tog, K1, P1) to end. 36 sts.

Work 13 rows K1, P1 rib.
Cast off in rib in C.
With ws facing, rejoin yarn to sts left on spare needle at neck edge and complete right front to match left front, reversing shapings.

POCKET LININGS AND EDGINGS
Work as given for Zigzag Jacket on page 63.

CUFFS
Using 5½mm (US 9) needles and yarn A, with rs facing K up 50 sts along edge of sleeve.
**Next row** P2, (P2 tog, P1) to end. 34 sts.
Work 15 rows K1, P1 rib.
Cast off in rib in C.

BUTTON BAND
Using 5½mm (US 9) needles and yarn A, with rs facing K up 98 sts (10 on rib, 88 on main part) along right front edge (for a man's jacket, left front edge for a woman's).
Work in diagonal rib as foll:
**1st row** P2, (K2, P2) to end.
**2nd row** K1, (P2, K2) to last st, P1.
**3rd row** K2, (P2, K2) to end.
**4th row** P1, (K2, P2) to last st, K1.
Rep 1st–2nd rows.
Cast off loosely in patt.

BUTTONHOLE BAND
Using 5½mm (US 9) needles and yarn A, with rs facing K up 98 sts as given for button band along left front edge (for a man's jacket, right front edge for a woman's).
    Work in diagonal rib as for button band making buttonholes on 3rd and 4th rows as foll:
**3rd row** Patt 3 sts, (cast off 2 sts, patt 13 sts including st used to cast off) 6 times, cast off 2 sts, patt to end.
**4th row** Patt to end, casting on 2 sts over those cast off in previous row.
Patt 2 rows.
Cast off in patt.

TO MAKE UP
Fold pocket edgings on to ws and catch down. Backstitch side and sleeve seams. Catch down pocket linings on to ws of fronts.
**Collar**
Using 5½mm (US 9) needles and yarn A, with rs facing K up 70 sts evenly round neck edge.
Work 14 rows K1, P1 rib.
Cast off in rib in C.

*(Overleaf) My belief in the beauty of tone on tone is clearly underlined in both of these pictures, from the smouldering ochres and yellows to the vibrant shades of blue in two wonderful Maltese settings for the yellow Star Jacket, the Star Coat and the Star Waistcoat.*

Stars

# Coat

The colouring of the Dark Star Coat (pages 95 and 98) reminds me now of early American patchwork quilts, though the original inspiration came from Caucasian carpets. I made it in chunky tweeds and heavy cotton chenilles, but you could use mohair, bouclé, plain wool or whatever you like.

You can use the same pattern to make the pastel version (opposite). These colours were inspired by an old chenille curtain I found in a flea market. Mossy greens, pinks and butter yellow, with touches of dusty sky blue and beige make a beautifully faded warm colour scheme. The yarns are mainly chenilles and wools.

About twenty-five colours are used in each coat. The main thing about these stars is to keep the colour changes fairly close in value, with half the star being a contrast (a very gentle one in some cases) to the other half. Each row of stars has a different outline.

## MATERIALS
Approx 2200g (78oz) total weight mixed yarns averaging chunky weight in three groups of colours—the background (A), the star outline (B) and the star (C)
1 pair each 4½mm (US 7), 5½mm (US 9) and 6½mm (US 10½) needles
9 buttons

## TENSION
15 sts and 16 rows to 10cm (4in) over patt on 6½mm (US 10½) needles.

## MEASUREMENTS
**To fit bust/chest** up to 111cm (44in)
**Actual width** 129cm (51in)
**Length to shoulder** 124cm (49in)
**Side seam** 81cm (32in)
**Sleeve seam** 51cm (20in)

## BACK, FRONTS AND SLEEVES (one piece)
Beg at lower back edge, using 5½mm (US 9) needles and chosen yarn, cast on 80 sts. Work 10 rows K1, P1 rib in stripes at random.
**Next row** Rib 2, K up loop between last st and next st to make 1, (rib 5, make 1) to last 3 sts, rib 2, make 1, rib 1. 97 sts.
Change to 6½mm (US 10½) needles and commence colour patt from chart, working in st st throughout, weaving yarns into back of work, as foll:
**1st row** (rs) K(8A, 1B, 15A, 1B, 7A) 3 times, 1A.
**2nd row** P1A, (7A, 2B, 13A, 2B, 8A) 3 times.
Cont in patt as set, changing background and star colours approx every 17 rows and outline colour every 34 rows, rep 1st–34th rows until 120 rows in all have been worked in colour patt (mark each end of 77th and 110th rows for pockets), ending with a ws row.
**Shape sleeves**
Cast on 64 sts at beg of next 2 rows (working 2 patt rep from chart across each new set of cast-on sts). 225 sts.
Work straight until 186 rows in all have been worked in colour patt, ending with a ws row.
**Divide for neck and fronts**
**Next row** Patt 100 sts, turn, leaving rem sts on spare needle and cont on these sts only for right side.
*Work 1 row (this point marks the shoulder line—reverse colour sequence from this point if you want fronts to match back).
Work 10 rows straight then inc 1 st at neck edge on next and every foll 4th row until there are 113 sts on needle.
Now work straight until front sleeve matches back from shoulder line, ending at sleeve edge.
**Shape sleeve**
Cast off 64 sts at beg of next row. 49 sts.
Now work straight until front matches back from shoulder line to top of rib, marking equivalent

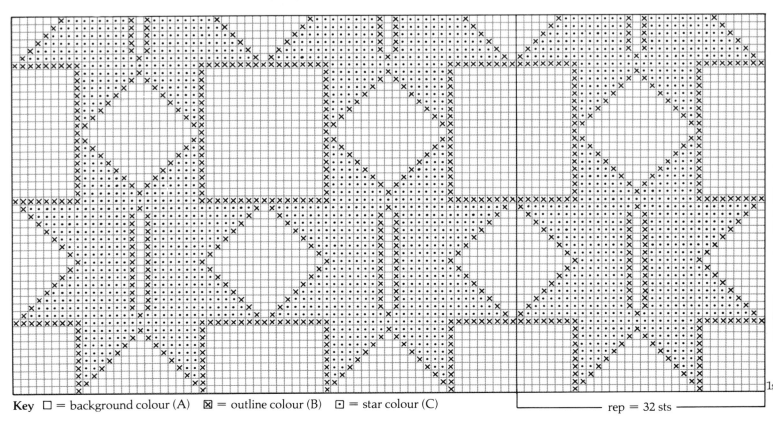

**Key** □ = background colour (A)  ⊠ = outline colour (B)  ⊡ = star colour (C)

rep = 32 sts

rows for pocket.
Change to 5½mm (US 9) needles and yarn as for back rib. Work in K1, P1 rib as foll:
**Next row** (K1, P1) twice, (K2 tog, P1, K1, P1) to end. 40 sts.
Rib 10 rows as for back.
Cast off in rib.
With rs facing rejoin yarn to sts on spare needle at neck edge, cast off 25 sts, patt to end.
Complete left side to match right, working from * to end.

POCKET LININGS AND EDGINGS
Work as given for Zigzag Jacket on page 63.

CUFFS
Using 5½mm (US 9) needles and yarn as for back rib, with rs facing K up 70 sts along sleeve edge.
Work 5 rows K1, P1 rib in stripes at random.
**Next row** (K1, P1) twice, K1, (P3 tog, K1, P1, K3 tog, P1, K1) to last 5 sts, (P1, K1) twice, P1. 46 sts.
Work 5 rows K1, P1 rib.
**Next row** K1, P1, K1, (P3 tog, K1, P1, K3 tog, P1, K1) to last 3 sts, P1, K1, P1. 30 sts.
Change to 4½mm (US 7) needles.

Work 6 rows K1, P1 rib.
Cast off in rib.

TO MAKE UP
Fold pocket edgings on to ws and catch down. Join side and sleeve seams. Catch down pocket linings on to ws of fronts.
**Front band**
Using 5½mm (US 9) needles and yarn as for back rib, with rs facing K up 342 sts around edge of right front, back neck and left front.
Work in diagonal rib in random stripes as foll:
**1st row** (ws) K2, (P2, K2) to end.
**2nd row** P1, (K2, P2) to last st, K1.
**3rd row** P2, (K2, P2) to end.
**4th row** K1, (P2, K2) to last st, P1.
These 4 rows form the patt rep.
Patt 1 row. Make buttonholes on next row as foll:
**Buttonhole row** Patt 3 sts, (cast off 2 sts, patt 12 sts including st used to cast off) 9 times, patt to end.
**Next row** Patt to end, casting on 2 sts over those cast off in previous row.
Patt 3 more rows. Cast off evenly in patt.
Sew on buttons.

*These two colour ideas for the star motif are quite different in effect. The coat uses springlike pastel tones. The pullover is in about ten shades of steely greys with highlights of turquoises and French blues. There isn't a pattern for this but you can try it on a three-colours-a-row pullover. The star is the same as the one on the child's sweater.*

*(Overleaf) The dark version of the Star Coat. This all-in-one kimino shape has a heavy drape. Both it and the waistcoat (page 100) are photographed in an abandoned villa in Malta.*

Stars

*(Far right) This is a good example of an intricate design which calls for the follow-through of a patterned buttonband. The star on the buttonband is essentially the same as the Circus Star motif. You could try this band on some of the other waistcoats or jackets for a jolly mixing of patterns. Photographed with the dark version of the Star Coat (page 96).*

# *Waistcoat*

You will notice that I usually contrast these stars with a light outline colour on both halves, so a deep rich background, like this navy, shows them up wonderfully. Any similar background colour—maroon or dark olive—will work just as well.

## MATERIALS
Approx 350g (13oz) mixed yarns and colours averaging double knitting weight
1 pair each 3¾mm (US 5) and 4½mm (US 7) needles

## TENSION
24 sts and 24 rows to 10cm (4in) over patt on 4½mm (US 7) needles.

## MEASUREMENTS
**To fit bust/chest** up to 96cm (38in)
**Actual width** 101cm (40in)
**Length to shoulder** 56cm (22in)
**Side seam** 32cm (12½in)

## BACK
Using 3¾mm (US 5) needles and chosen yarn, cast on 121 sts.
Work 10 rows st st, beg with a P row.
K 1 row to form hemline.
Change to 4½mm (US 7) needles and commence colour patt from chart 1, working in st st throughout, weaving yarns into back of work, as foll:
**1st row** (rs) K4C, 1B, 1A, 1B, 3C, (4C, 1B, 1A, 1B, 7C, 1B, 1A, 1B, 3C) 5 times, 4C, 1B, 1A, 1B, 4C.
**2nd row** As 1st row but P instead of K.
Cont in patt as set changing background and star colours about halfway up each star and outline colour from star to star, until 44 rows have been worked from chart. Now rep 25th–44th rows until 76 rows in all have been worked from hemline row, ending with a ws row.**

## Shape armholes
Cast off 5 sts at beg of next 2 rows, then dec 1 st at each end of foll 4 rows, now dec 1 st at each end of every alt row until 95 sts rem.
Work straight until 134 rows have been worked from hemline row, ending with a ws row.
## Shape shoulders
Cast off 7 sts at beg of next 6 rows. 53 sts.
Cast off.

## LEFT FRONT
Using 3¾mm (US 5) needles and chosen yarn, cast on 61 sts.
Work as given for back to **, working between front markers on chart.
## Shape armholes and front neck
Cast off 5 sts at beg of next row, then dec 1 st at armhole edge on foll 4 rows, then 1 st at armhole edge on foll 4 alt rows, *at the same time* dec 1 st at front edge on next and every alt row until 21 sts rem.
Work straight until front matches back to shoulder, ending at armhole edge.
## Shape shoulder
Cast off 7 sts at beg of next and foll alt row. Work 1 row.
Cast off rem 7 sts.

## RIGHT FRONT
Work as given for left front, reversing shapings by working 1 more row before shaping armhole.

## TO MAKE UP
Backstitch shoulder seams.
## Armbands
Using 4½mm (US 7) needles and chosen yarn, with rs facing K up 125 sts around armhole edge.
Work 2 rows st st, beg with a P row.
K 2 rows to form foldline.
Work 6 rows st st, beg with a P row. Cast off.
Join side seams. Fold hem and armbands on to ws and catch down.
## Front band
Using 4½mm (US 7) needles and chosen yarn, with rs facing K up 125 sts up right front edge, 51 sts across back neck and 125 sts down left front edge. 301 sts.
Commence colour patt from chart 2, working in st st and beg with a P row, keeping background colours constant and changing star colours as required, work 1st–9th rows.
P 2 rows to form foldline.
Work 10 rows st st, beg with a K row.
Cast off loosely.
Fold front band on to ws and catch down.

☐ = background colour (A)
☒ = outline colour (B)
⊡ = star colour (C)

**Chart 1**

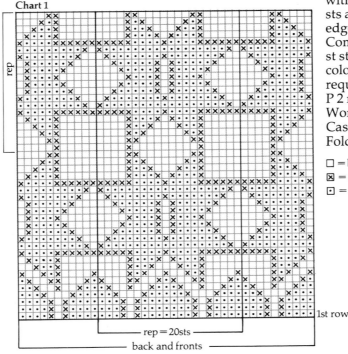

rep = 20sts
back and fronts

**Chart 2**

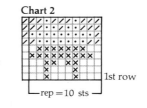

1st row
rep = 10 sts

# SQUARES & PATCHES

The square is the most basic of geometric shapes. There is something immensely pleasing about its evenness. The sides being as long as the top and bottom brings a sense of security—no surprises. A square in the middle of a richly complex design can be dramatically calm and strong.

There's plenty of inspiration for square-based designs in the ordinary world around us. Squares are everywhere, in many colourings and on scales from tiny to huge. Piles of brick ends are a favourite of mine. Their dusty tones of different coloured clays make a perfect subject for a fabric design. They did, in fact, inspire the colouring for Little Squares (see page 123). But there are hundreds of other things that we see constantly that could provide just such a spark—mosaic boxes, tiled floors, chess boards, graph paper and so on.

Let's take the chess board as an example. This is the perfect starter to get the feel of two-colour knitting. Play with scale. Start off with black and beige or a lighter colour. Work two stitches of each alternately for two rows. For the next two rows change the position of the colours and you have your checks. Now work it with four stitches over four rows and so on up to twenty stitches or more. This will help you get the feel of differences in scale—from fine texture to bold drama. Then you can play with putting these blocks in a different arrangement. Try it out on graph paper, putting ticks in that lovely square grid.

The idea for patches first occurred to me when I was searching for a way to show the impact of colours as they appear in a basket of yarn hanks. Often I'd be moved by great chunks of colour in balls and hanks, only to find the effect quite dissipated by small fragmented Fair Isle designs. By building up the colour in blocks you keep that original impact.

The traditional appeal of patchwork was also strong. Travelling in Afghanistan and Pakistan, I saw amazingly patched clothes being washed in the rivers and then laid out to dry on the rocks and was delighted by the beauty of the faded tones. The sight of patched oriental robes of richly patterned fabrics also stayed in my mind. Closer to home, I love those patched tarpaulins that are hung up on buildings being cleaned, and in rusting corrugated metal you get the same wonderful range of shades in bold patches of colour.

*(Far left) This is my patchwork sampler showing my first colour and pattern experiments. I crocheted round each swatch in shades of grey and added several rows round the whole sampler to make a richly patterned luxurious bedspread. The Squares Shawl (page 107) and a swatch of the Carpet Pattern (page 40) in a grey colouring are pinned to the wall. You can also see the Lattice V-neck Sweater (page 118) worn with an antique Afghani cotton skirt.*

# Crosspatch

Every nation on earth has its version of plaid. Think of the fabrics in Japanese prints and of Scottish tartans for a start. This is my homage to that timeless pattern. It has the simplicity of overall solid shapes, but they are broken by fine slivers of colour—simple and complex at the same time.

To me the design suggests tiles or boxes tied with two-colour ribbons (imagine designing a sweater by tying ribbons on to different coloured tiles—think of how many different ways you could tie those ribbons).

By the way, if you're daunted by the idea of knitting all those fine vertical lines, you can always Swiss-darn them on afterwards.

## Sleeveless Pullover

The grey and beige version given in the pattern, knitted in a fine tweed yarn throughout, is a favourite of mine. For the dark version substitute a range of forest greens, browns, maroons, deep navy and add some medium contrasts of beige, rust and so on. This design knitted in chunky yarns on one of the jacket patterns (Large Step Jacket on page 54, for instance) would look gorgeous.

### MATERIALS
**Yarn used**
75g (3oz) Rowan Yarns Light Tweed each in silver 208 (A) and charcoal 210 (C); 50g (2oz) each in grey 209 (B), autumn 205 (D), ebony 207 (F), lakeland 222 (G) and atlantic 223 (H); 25g (1oz) each in pebble 203 (E) and lavender 213 (J)
**Equivalent yarn** four-ply
1 pair each 2¾mm (US 2) and 3¼mm (US 3) needles
1 set four double-pointed 2¾mm (US 2) needles (or circular needle)

(Far right) *The grey colourway specified in the pattern. These very neutral tweedy tones look particularly good against a wonderful background of ceanothus in Kew Gardens, London. The dark version (right) reminds me of old Japanese woodcuts. Both these colourings are very muted in approach but this design could also be a vehicle for a riot of colours.*

### TENSION
24 sts and 36 rows to 10cm (4in) over patt on 3¼mm (US 3) needles.

### SIZE
**To fit chest/bust** up to 96cm (38in)
**Actual width** 102cm (40in)
**Length to shoulder** 63cm (25in)
**Side seam** 40cm (16in)

### BACK
Using 2¾mm (US 2) needles and yarn C, cast on 121 sts.
Work in K1, P1 rib as foll: 8 rows in C, 2 rows in G, 1 row in A, 2 rows in G, 7 rows in C (inc 1 st at end of last row). 122 sts.
Change to 3¼mm (US 3) needles and commence colour patt from chart on page 106, working in st st throughout, use separate strands of yarn for each block of colours and twist them together between colours to avoid holes:
**1st row** (rs) K12D, 1F, 1G, 1F, 8D, 8G, 1A, 1H, 1A, 8G, 8F, 1H, 1E, 1H, 8F, 8B, 1E, 1F, 1E, 8B, 8H, 1A, 1C, 1A, 8H, 8A, 1F, 1G, 1F, 12A.
**2nd row** P to end using same colours as previous row.
Cont in patt as set, working each block of colour as indicated by code letters on chart itself, and vertical and horizontal crosses foll chart key for symbols, work 126 rows in all from chart, ending with a ws row.
**Shape armholes**
Cast off 12 sts at beg of next 2 rows, then dec 1 st at each end of next and every alt row until 86 sts rem, ending with a ws row.**
Work straight until 210 patt rows in all have been completed, thus ending with a ws row.
**Shape shoulders**
Cast off 6 sts at beg of next 2 rows, then 7 sts at beg of foll 4 rows. 46 sts. Cast off.

### FRONT
Work as for back to **.
**Divide for neck**
**Next row** Patt 41 sts, K2 tog, turn, leaving rem sts on a spare needle and cont on these sts only for left side of neck. 42 sts.
Work 2 rows.
Dec 1 st at neck edge on next and every alt row until 31 sts rem, then on every foll 4th row until 20 sts rem. Work straight until front matches back to shoulder, ending at armhole edge.
**Shape shoulder**
Cast off 6 sts at beg of next row and 7 sts at beg of foll alt row. Work 1 row. Cast off rem 7 sts.
With rs facing, rejoin yarn to neck edge, K2 tog, patt to end. 42 sts.
Complete right side to match left reversing shapings.

### TO MAKE UP
Backstitch shoulder seams.
**Neckband**
Using double-pointed 2¾mm (US 2) needles and yarn C, with rs facing K up 82 sts down left front

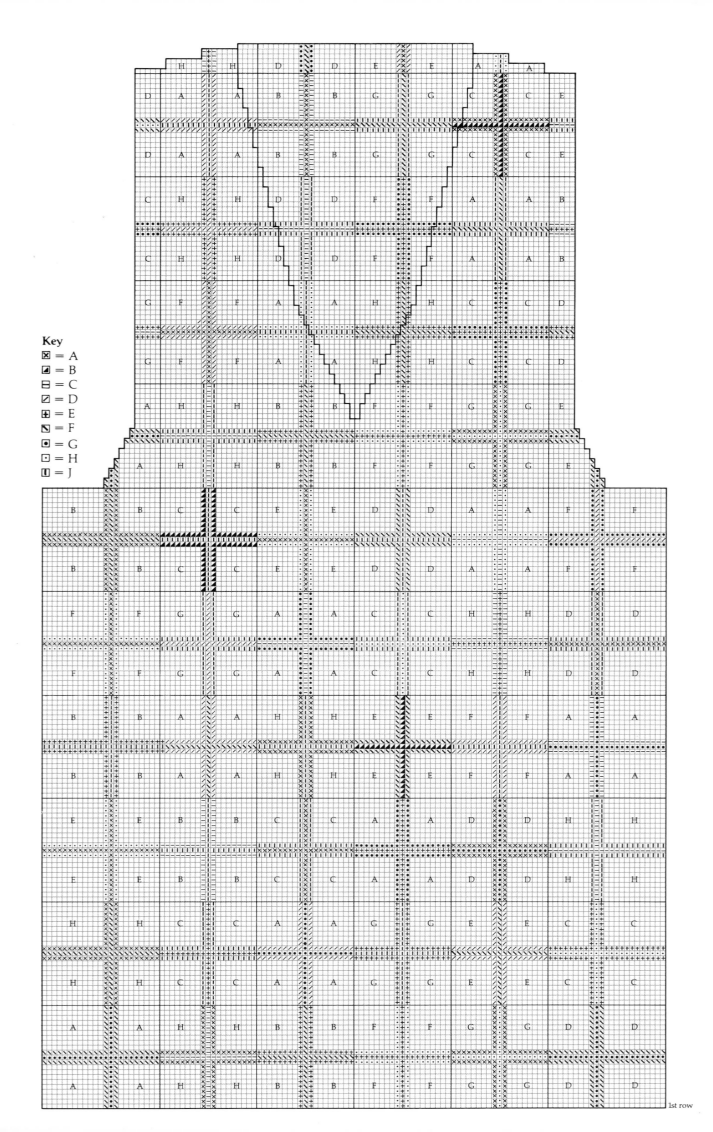

**Key**

⊠ = A
◪ = B
⊟ = C
◪ = D
⊞ = E
◩ = F
⊡ = G
⊡ = H
Ⅲ = J

1st row

neck, 1 st at centre front V, 82 sts up right front neck and 49 sts from back neck. 214 sts.

Work in K1, P1 rib in rounds as foll:

**1st round** Rib to with 2 sts of centre st, K2 tog tbl, K1, K2 tog, rib to end of round.

Cont in rib in this way, dec 1 st on each side of centre st and K centre st on every round, as foll: 2 rounds in C, 1 round in G, 1 round in A, 1 round in G and 3 rounds in C.

Cast off in C in rib, dec at centre front as before.

**Armbands**

Using 2¾mm (US 2) needles and yarn B, with rs facing, K up 172 sts around armhole edge.

Work in K1, P1 rib as foll:

2 rows in B, 2 rows in C.

Cast off loosely in rib in C.

Join side seams.

# Squares Shawl

The simple desire to do every variation of scale on a square led to this most intricate of designs. I just cast on my three stitches as usual for my shawls and, picking many tones of cream and sandstone colours, placed one square after another on a medium grey ground.

I set myself the restraint of never letting more than a stitch or row of the background show, if at all. This gives the design its compact texture. The little touches of colour in the centres are kept quite soft to tone in with the warm stone colours. I've often thought of a Middle Eastern village nestled on a hill—blocks of creamy houses with the occasional pastel one would make an excellent subject.

# Coat

After the regularity of the Crosspatch Pullover, it was only a matter of time before the idea of changing scale and colour produced this coat. The pattern of overlapping squares in various sizes divided by two-colour crosses is completely invented as you go along on a basic coat shape (the Carpet Coat on page 42 would be suitable if you want to try this one).

I started the back with five different sized squares, each with their cross colours. You must use manageable lengths of yarn for working this design. You can carry the outline cross colour across the centre colour if you like, as I do (Zoë likes to have two separate threads, so that the knitting lies flatter), but otherwise use separate lengths of yarn for each block of colour and work them by the intarsia method.

Knit up your squares, interrupting them at different points with new patches. I watch carefully to see that none of the cross bars line up with each other. You can make the fronts a mirror image of the back, as here, or carry on inventing new patches (be aware, coming down the fronts, of what will happen at the side seams when the coat is made up; avoid any same-colour joins, unless that is what you want).

The colours in this one are all fairly muted, with accents of black and periwinkle. I wanted to create a coat that was dynamically patterned but tweedy enough to tone in anywhere. A very dark colour scheme (like the one on the Crosspatch Pullover on page 104) would be extremely handsome—purples, blacks, deep greens and tweedy maroons. I can also envisage a shell-like colouring—silver greys, creams, lavenders and cool beiges—similar to that of the Squares Shawl (page 107). Be careful not to have any colours that are too 'hot' in your range. Often one is tempted to use pinks or beiges that detract from the faded shell look.

(Below) *This is the layout of the back of my version of the Crosspatch Coat. I just wanted to show you how this improvised design ended up. Rather than following such a plan it's much less daunting to invent your own scheme as you go along. Don't be afraid to employ dramatic leaps in scale.*

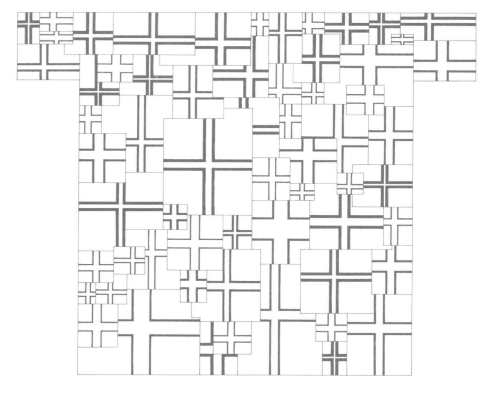

# Ribbon Design

The woven effect of this ribbon design really fascinates me, and it's a superb vehicle for colour arrangements. To plan your colourways you can weave strips of coloured paper together or just lay hanks of coloured yarns across each other to see how they 'read' or work together.

On most of my weave-look designs (see also the Lattice designs on pages 118–20) I try to send the warmer colours in from one side with the cooler colours coming from the opposite direction. This way you don't get those 'melting in' surprises when two crossing colours are so close in tone that they read as the same colour.

## V-neck Sweater

These ribbon designs are marvellous to knit. The dark background squares after every horizontal band seem to act as a punctuation mark and a spur to finish just one more ribbon!

When carrying the yarns for the horizontal ribbons across the back, always take the yarn to the end of each row, even if it's not needed. This gives a more even texture to the finished garment.

### MATERIALS
Approx 50[75]g (2[3]oz) mixed yarns averaging chunky weight in each of seven vertical ribbon colours (A, B, C, D, E, F, G)
Approx 50g (2oz) in each of thirteen horizontal ribbon colours (H, J, L, M, N, P, Q, R, S, T, U, V, W)
Approx 50g (2oz) in squares colour Y
1 pair each 5mm (US 8) and 6mm (US 10) needles

### TENSION
16 sts and 20 rows to 10cm (4in) over patt on 6mm (US 10) needles.

(Overleaf) *The colours in this version of the Ribbon V-neck Sweater have a particular Italianate quality. None of these soft, sun-baked tones are at all bright or harsh. The medium blue background squares simply emphasize the softness of the 'ribbons'. It's photographed with the Carpet Pullover (page 40). The luminous pastels of the other colourway (inset and right) show how versatile this design can be. The deep dark background colour gives the jewel-like 'ribbons' an almost three-dimensional quality.*

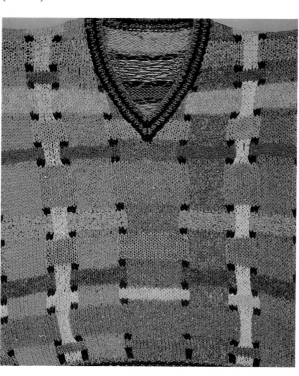

### MEASUREMENTS
**To fit bust/chest** 81–91[96–106]cm (32–36[38–42]in)
**Actual width** 111[124]cm (44[48½]in)
**Length to shoulder** 60[64]cm (23½[25½]in)
**Side seam** 40[43]cm (16[17]in)
**Sleeve seam** 46[51]cm (18[20]in)

### BACK
Using 5mm (US 8) needles and yarn A, cast on 76[86] sts.
*Work in K1, P1 rib as foll: 1 row A, (2 rows Y, 2 rows A) twice, 2 rows Y.*
**Next row** With A, rib 2[7], K up loop between last st and next st to make 1, (rib 6, make 1) to last 2[7] sts, rib 2[7]. 89[99] sts.
**Next row** P to end in A.
Change to 6mm (US 10) needles and commence colour patt from chart, working in st st throughout—weave yarns for horizontal ribbons and Y into the back of the work, use separate lengths of yarn for each vertical ribbon and carry the yarn up the back of the work until needed on the next row—as foll:
**1st row** (rs) K2A [2Y, 5A], 2Y, 11B, 2Y, 5C, 2Y, 11D, 2Y, 15E, 2Y, 11F, 2Y, 5G, 2Y, 11A, 2Y, 2G [5G, 2Y].
**2nd row** Read 1st row in reverse but P instead of K in the stated colours.
Cont in patt as set, working vertical ribbons in same colours throughout and colours indicated on chart for horizontal ribbons, until 70[76] rows in all have been worked from chart.**
### Shape armholes
Keeping patt correct, cast off 9 sts at beg of next 2 rows. 71[81] sts.
Cont in ribbon patt until 110[118] rows in all have been worked from chart, thus ending with a ws row.
### Shape shoulders
Cast off 8[9] sts at beg of next 4 rows and 7[9] sts at beg of foll 2 rows.
Leave rem 25[27] sts on a spare needle.

### FRONT
Work as given for back to **.
### Shape armholes and divide for neck
**Next row** Cast off 9 sts, patt 35[40] sts including st used to cast off, K2 tog, patt to end. 79[89] sts.
**Next row** Cast off 9 sts, patt 35[40] sts including st used to cast off, turn, leaving rem sts on a spare needle and cont on these sts only for right side of neck. 35[40] sts.
Work 1 row.***
Now dec 1 st at neck edge on next and every foll 3rd row until 23[27] sts rem.
Cont in patt without shaping until work matches the back to beg of shoulder shaping, ending at armhole edge.
### Shape shoulder
Cast off 8[9] sts at beg of next and foll alt row.
Work 1 row. Cast off rem 7[9] sts.
Rejoin yarns to sts on spare needle.
Work 2 rows, then complete left side to match right from *** to end.

Ribbon Design

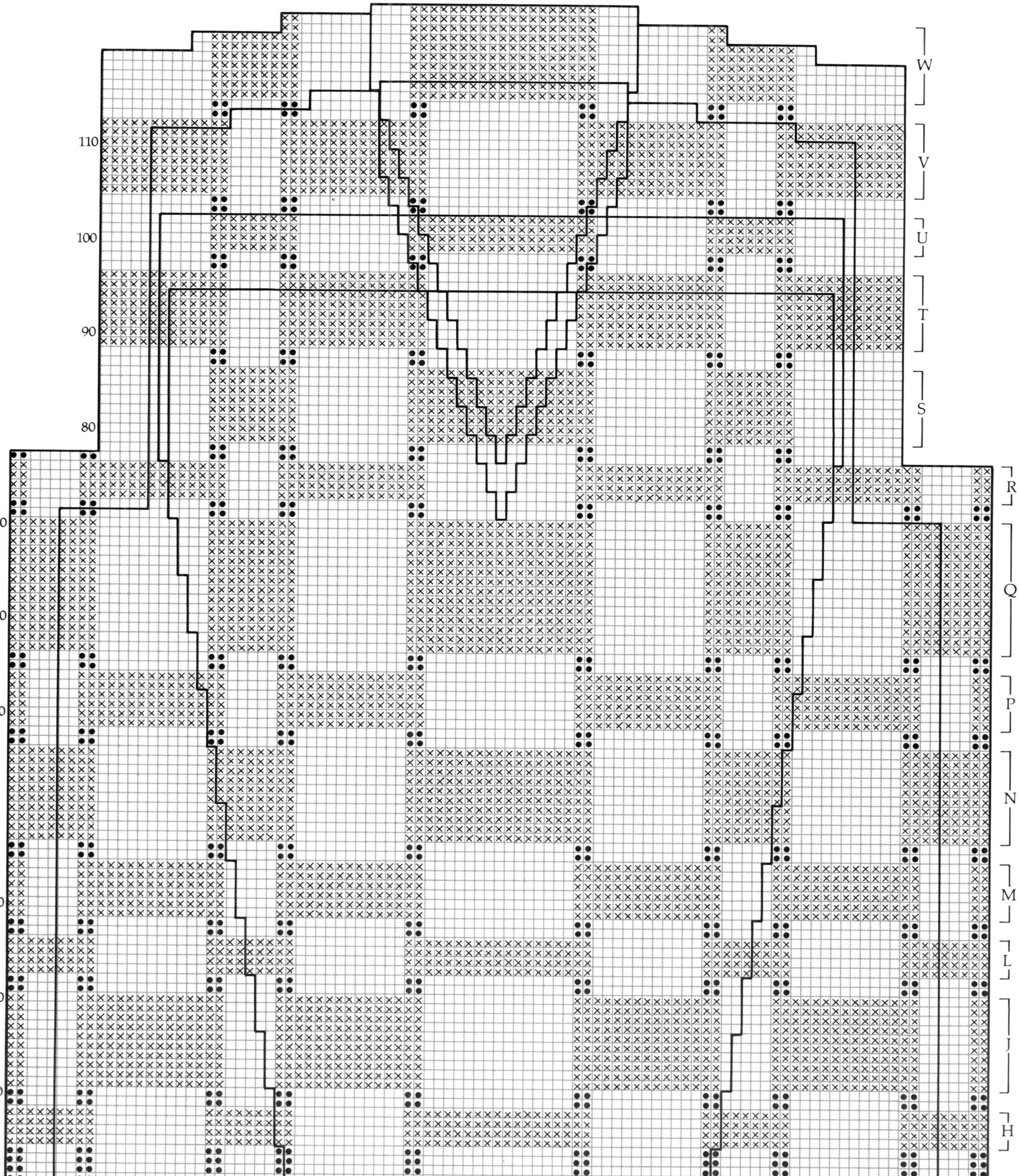

W

V

U

110

T

100

S

90

80

R

Q

P

N

M

L

J

H

1st row

┌G┐ ┌────A────┐ ┌G┐ ┌────F────┐ ┌────E────┐ ┌────D────┐ ┌──C──┐ ┌────B────┐ ┌A┐

size | 1st size | 2nd size ... 1st size | 2nd size

sleeve

back and front

**Key**  □ = vertical ribbons   ⊠ = horizontal ribbons   ⊡ = Y throughout

## SLEEVES

Using 5mm (US 8) needles and yarn A, cast on 34 sts.

Work in K1, P1 rib as given for back from * to *.

**Next row** With A, rib 5, make 1, (rib 3, make 1) to last 5 sts, rib to end. 43 sts.

Change to 6mm (US 10) needles and commence colour patt from chart working between sleeve markers, *at the same time* inc 1 st at each end of 5th and every foll 6th row until there are 65[69] sts. Now work straight until 94[102] rows in all have been worked from chart.

Cast off.

## TO MAKE UP

Backstitch left shoulder seam.

**Neckband**

Using 5mm (US 8) needles and yarn Y, with rs facing K across 25[27] sts at back neck, K up 45[47] sts down left front neck and 45[47] sts up right front neck. 115[121] sts.

Work in K1, P1 rib as foll:

**1st row** Rib 43[45], P2 tog, P2 tog tbl, rib to end.

**2nd row** With A, rib 67[71], K2 tog tbl, K2 tog, rib to end.

Rib 5 more rows (1 row A, 2 rows Y, 2 rows A), dec at front neck as set, knitwise on rs rows and purlwise on ws rows.

Cast off in rib, dec as before at front neck.

Backstitch right shoulder seam.

Set sleeves in flat, matching centre of cast-off edge of sleeve to shoulder seam and joining last few rows of sleeve to cast-off sts at underarm.

Backstitch side and sleeve seams.

# Child's Sweater

This is a scaled-down version of the adult sweater, in double knitting rather than chunky yarn.

The blue-grey colourway was invented at the same time as the Striped-patch Pullover (page 122), when I was in love with those frosty blues and greys. The pastels version (right) is the one specified in the pattern.

## MATERIALS

**Yarns used**

75g (3oz) Rowan Yarns Double Knitting Wool in blue/grey 88 (A); 25g (1oz) each in biscuit 104 (B), pale pink 109 (C), fawn 82 (E), flesh pink 615 (G), mauve 92 (H), silver blue 64 (J), yellow/green 31 (L), mauve 69 (M), nile green 416 (Q), pale peach 103 (S), tea 86 (U), beige 614 (V) and pink 68 (W); 25[50]g (1[2]oz) in silver 58 (X)

25g (1oz) Rowan Yarns Light Tweed each in bracken 204 (D), silver 208 (F), rosemix 215 (N), grey 209 (R) and lavender 213 (T)

**Equivalent yarn** double knitting

1 pair each 3¼mm (US 3) and 4mm (US 6) needles

## TENSION

24 sts and 32 rows to 10cm (4in) over patt on 4mm (US 6) needles.

## MEASUREMENTS

**To fit chest** 71[76]cm (28[30]in)

**Actual width** 75[81]cm (29½[32]in)

*(Overleaf) The cool blues and warm pastels of the Ribbon Sweaters are beautifully reflected in Richard Womersley's woven rug and little squares sampler. The small cushion on the left is an early work of mine in petit point.*

**Length to shoulder** 39[40]cm (15[15½]in)

**Side seam** 25cm (10in)

**Sleeve seam** 33[35]cm (13[14]in)

## BACK

Using 3¼mm (US 3) needles and yarn A, cast on 80[85] sts.

Work in K1, P1 rib as foll: (2 rows in A, 2 rows in F) 4 times, 1 row in A.

**Next row** With A, rib 7[4], (K up loop between next st and last st to make 1, rib 6[7]) 11 times, make 1, rib to end. 91[97] sts.

**Next row** P to end in A.

Change to 4mm (US 6) needles and commence colour patt from chart, working in st st throughout (carry yarns for horizontal ribbons and A across the back of the work weaving them in as you go; use separate lengths of yarn for each vertical ribbon weaving in on one st each side of each ribbon and carrying the yarn up the back of the work until needed on the next row), as foll:

**1st row** (rs) K3[6]B, 2A, 11C, 2A, 5D, 2A, 11E, 2A, 15F, 2A, 11G, 2A, 5H, 2A, 11J, 2A, 3[6]L.

**2nd row** As 1st row in reverse but P instead of K using the appropriate colours.

Cont in patt as set, working vertical ribbons in same colours throughout and colours indicated on chart for horizontal ribbons. Work 64 rows in all from chart, thus ending with a P row.

**Shape armholes**

Cast off 8 sts at beg of next 2 rows. 75[81] sts.**

Cont in patt until 106[110] rows have been worked from chart.

**Shape shoulders**

Cast off 6 sts at beg of next 2 rows. 63[69] sts.

**Divide for neck**

**Next row** Cast off 6 sts, patt 15[18] sts, cast off 21 sts, patt to end.

**Next row** Cast off 6 sts, patt to neck edge, turn, leaving rem sts on a spare needle and cont on these sts only for left side of neck. 15[18] sts.
Cast off 3 sts at beg of next row, then 6 sts at beg of foll row and 2[3] sts at beg of next row.
Cast off rem 4[6] sts.
With ws facing rejoin yarn to neck edge and complete right side to match left, reversing shapings.

FRONT
Work as given for back to **.
**Divide for neck**
**Next row** Patt 36[39] sts, K2 tog, turn, leaving rem sts on a spare needle and cont on these sts only for left side of neck. 37[40] sts.
Work 2 rows straight.
Dec 1 st at neck edge on next and every foll 3rd row until 24[26] sts rem, ending at armhole edge.
**Shape shoulder**
Cast off 6 sts at beg of next and foll 2 alt rows, *at the same time* cont to dec at neck edge on 3rd rows as before.
Cast off rem 4[6] sts.
With rs facing, rejoin yarn to neck edge and complete right side to match left, reversing shapings.

SLEEVES
Using 3¼mm (US 3) needles and yarn A, cast on 35 sts.
Work 17 rows K1, P1 rib in colours as for back.
**Next row** With A, rib 4, (make 1, rib 4) 7 times, make 1, rib to end. 43 sts.
Change to 4mm (US 6) needles and commence colour patt from chart, working between sleeve markers as foll:
**1st row** (rs) K1A, 11E, 2A, 15F, 2A, 11G, 1A.
**2nd row** As 1st row in reverse but P instead of K.
Cont in patt as set, *at the same time* inc 1 st at each end of every 5th chart row until there are 63[69] sts.
Now work straight until sleeve measures 36[38]cm (14[15]in). Cast off.

TO MAKE UP
Backstitch left shoulder seam.
**Neckband**
Using 3¼mm (US 3) needles and yarn A, with rs of work facing, K up 35[37] sts around back neck, 40[42] sts down left side of neck, 1 st at centre front and 40[42] sts up right side of neck. 116[122] sts.
Work in K1, P1 rib.
**1st row** Rib 38[40], P2 tog, P1, P2 tog tbl, rib to end. 114[120] sts.
**2nd row** With F, rib to within 2 sts of centre st, K2 tog tbl, K1, K2 tog, rib to end. 112[118] sts.
Cont to dec each side of centre st in this way, working purlwise decs on ws rows and knitwise decs on rs rows, rib 7 more rows as foll: 1 row in F, 2 rows in A, 2 rows in F, 2 rows in A.
Cast off in rib in A.
Backstitch left shoulder seam.
Set sleeves in flat using a backstitch seam, matching centre of cast-off edge to shoulder seam and joining last few rows of sleeve to cast-off sts at underarm.
Join side and sleeve seams.

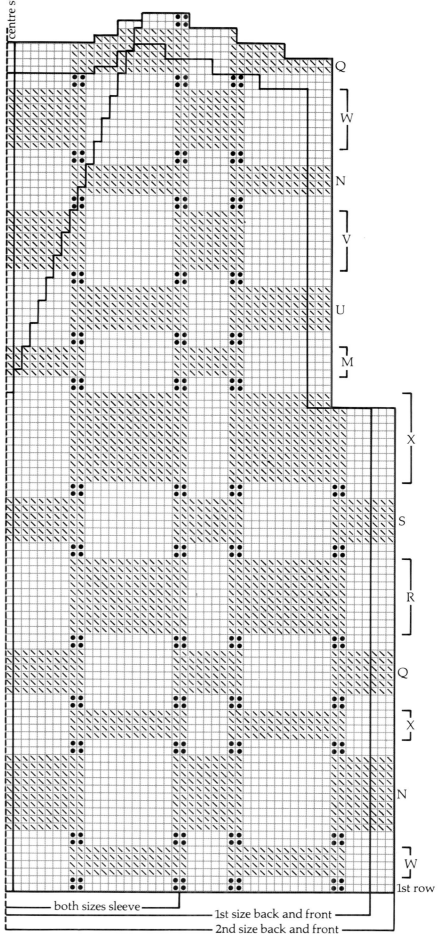

**Key** ▣ = A throughout  ☐ = vertical ribbons  ◩ = horizontal ribbons

**Note:** *the pattern layout is symmetrical. Using colours as set and reading from right to left, work each row to centre st, work centre st, then read chart in reverse to end of row, ignoring centre st.*

115

# Lattice Pattern

This is another of my weave-look designs (see also the Ribbon sweaters for hints on choosing colours for this kind of design). Some of the garments have changing background colours, others—and it's probably easier this way—have a solid colour background. If you are feeling adventurous, do experiment with the richness of changing background colours as it does add a certain subtlety to the design.

## Shawl

Here the ribbon design is worked on the classic triangular shawl pattern given on page 15. I aimed at a very brooding Celtic mood, using a muted palette. You can work a few rows from one of the ribbon graphs to get yourself started, and then improvise your own verticals and horizontals. Keep the horizontals to even numbers of rows so that the background and verticals yarns are in the right position for working the next row.

The dark background squares are kept constant throughout and, to make life easy, I also kept each horizontal ribbon a solid colour. However, on the vertical ribbons I built up variations in tone to add richness and movement. It also makes it more interesting to knit if you change colours now and again.

I used a set of cool colours for the horizontals (about eighteen blues and greys) and warm colours for the verticals (about nineteen shades of browns, rusts and plum tones), punctuated by dark charcoal background squares. Many variations on this are possible: what about dark rich colours, or all reds and rusts, or shell tones? For a really authentic patchwork look, try striped or patterned ribbons instead of plain ones.

*To give this design an entirely different feeling you could make the background colour a light creamy tone with crossed bands of medium pastels, for instance, pinks, sage greens, sky blues and warm beiges, like an old English chintz (see page 123).*

## V-neck Sweater

These colours with their tweedy look remind me of flecked granite. If you substitute your own colours in this design, be careful that the colours coming from the right do not merge with those coming from the left. It should still be possible to keep them close in tone to create the tweedy effect I was after. Using pastel colours on a light cream background creates a springlike feeling.

MATERIALS
**Yarns used**
100[125]g (4[5]oz) Rowan Spun Tweed each in caviar 760 (A) and fig 761 (B); 50g (2oz) each in tea 752 (C), caper 762 (D) and tobacco 751 (E)
100g (4oz) Rowan Yarns Light Tweed in grey 209 (H); 75g (3oz) each in rosemix 215 (G) and atlantic 223 (J); 50g (2oz) in autumn 205 (F)
50g (2oz) Rowan Yarns Double Knitting Wool in grey 59 (L); 25[50]g (1[2]oz) in brown 616 (M); 25g (1oz) each in beige 613 (N) and midnight blue 65 (Q)
75g (3oz) Rowan Yarns Fine Cotton Chenille in shark 378 (S); 25g (1oz) each in steel 382 (R) and mole 380 (U)
25g (1oz) Rowan Yarns Cotton Chenille in ash beige 353 (T)
**Equivalent yarn** Aran/medium-weight
1 pair each 4½mm (US 7) and 5½mm (US 9) needles

NOTE
*The finer yarns are used in combination. For example, 'RF' means one strand each of yarns R and F; 'FHH' means one strand of F and two of H. If preferred Aran-weight yarns used singly can be substituted for the combined yarns throughout.*

TENSION
17 sts and 22 rows to 10cm (4in) over st st on 5½mm (US 9) needles.

MEASUREMENTS
**To fit bust/chest** 91–97[101–106]cm (36–38[40–42]in)
**Actual width** 108[120]cm (43[47½]in)
**Length to shoulder** 66[68]cm (26[27]in)
**Side seam** 42cm (16½in)
**Sleeve seam** 45[47]cm (17½[18½]in)

BACK
Using 4½mm (US 7) needles and yarns RF, cast on 80[88] sts.
Work in K1, P1 rib as foll: 2 rows in A, 1 row in FG, 14 rows in B.
**Next row** With B, rib 7[5], K up loop between last st and next st to make 1, (rib 6, make 1) to last st, rib 7[5]. 92[102] sts.
Change to 5½mm (US 9) needles and commence colour patt from chart on page 120, work in st st twisting yarns between colours to prevent holes (do not carry yarns across the back), as foll:
**1st row** (rs) K7[12]C, 6A, 12D, 6A, 12RF, 6A, 12B, 6A, 12E, 6A, 7[12]FHH.

# Squares & Patches

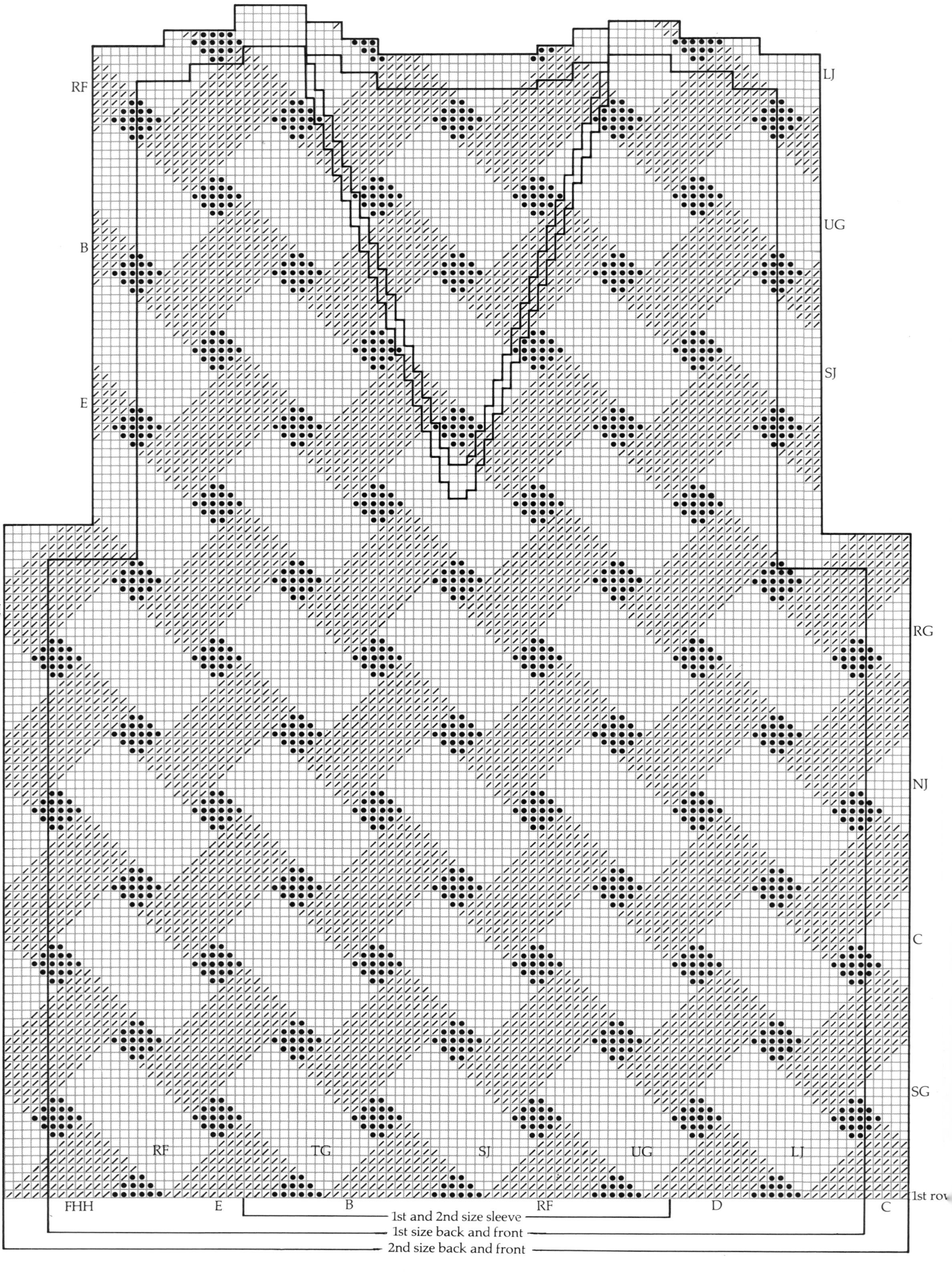

RF

LJ

B

UG

E

SJ

HHH

RG

QJ

NJ

MH

C

B

SG

SG RF TG SJ UG LJ

FHH E B RF D C 1st row

1st and 2nd size sleeve
1st size back and front
2nd size back and front

**2nd row** P8FHH [1SG, 12FHH], 4A, 2RF, 12E, 4A, 2TG, 12B, 4A, 2SJ, 12RF, 4A, 2UG, 12D, 4A, 2LJ, 6[11]C.

Cont in patt as set, keeping each diagonal 'strip' in the same colour throughout and foll colour code at sides of chart for new 'strips', work 74[78] rows, thus ending with a P row.

**Shape armholes**

Cast off 10 sts at beg of next 2 rows. 72[82] sts.*
Work 54 rows without shaping, ending with a P row.

**Shape shoulders and divide for neck**

**Next row** Cast off 6[8] sts, patt 21[24] sts including st used to cast off, cast off 18 sts, patt to end.

**Next row** Cast off 6[8] sts, patt to neck edge, turn, leaving rem sts on a spare needle and cont on these sts only for left side of neck. 21[24] sts.
Cast off 4 sts at beg of next row, then 6[8] sts at beg of foll row and 4 sts at beg of foll row.
Cast off rem 7[8] sts.
With ws facing, rejoin yarn to sts on spare needle at neck edge and complete right side to match left side, reversing shapings.

FRONT

Work as given for back to *.
Work 6 rows without shaping, ending with a P row.

**Divide for neck**

**Next row** Patt 34[39] sts, K2 tog, K2 tog tbl, patt to end.

**Next row** Patt 35[40] sts, turn, leaving rem sts on a spare needle and cont on these sts only for right side of neck.
Dec 1 st at neck edge on next and every foll 3rd row until there are 19[24] sts.
Work 1 row without shaping, thus ending at armhole edge.

**Shape shoulder**

Cast off 6[8] sts at beg of next and foll alt row.

Work 1 row.
Cast off rem 7[8] sts.
With ws facing, rejoin yarn to sts on spare needle at neck edge and complete left side to match right side, reversing shapings.

SLEEVES

Using 4½mm (US 7) needles and yarns RF, cast on 42 sts.
Work in K1, P1 rib as given for back.
**Next row** Rib 6, (make 1, rib 6) 6 times. 48 sts.
Change to 5½mm (US 9) needles and commence colour patt from chart working between sleeve markers, *at the same time* inc 1 st at each end of every 4th row until there are 76 sts, and then at each end of every 6th row until there are 84 sts.
Now work straight until sleeve measures 51[53]cm (20[21]in).
Cast off.

TO MAKE UP

Backstitch right shoulder seam.

**Neckband**

Using 4½mm (US 7) needles and yarn B, with rs facing, K up 48 sts down left side of neck, 1 st from centre front, 48 sts up right side of neck and 38 sts across back neck. 135 sts.
Work in K1, P1 rib as foll:
**Next row** Rib to within 2 sts of centre st, P2 tog, P1, P2 tog tbl, rib to end.
**Next row** Rib to within 2 sts of centre st, K2 tog tbl, K1, K2 tog tbl, rib to end.
Cont in this way, dec each side of centre st, purlwise on ws rows and knitwise on rs rows, rib 4 more rows in B, 1 row in FG, 2 rows in A.
Cast off in RF, dec as before.
Backstitch left shoulder seam.
Set sleeves in flat, matching centre of cast-off edge of sleeve to shoulder seam and joining last few rows of sleeve to cast-off sts at underarm.
Backstitch side and sleeve seams.

*I've used several different schemes on the Lattice Pattern. These two, on a crew-neck and boat-neck sweater, would work just as well on the V-neck. The red and blue colours were inspired by the red garden at Hidcote Manor in Gloucestershire, England. The crew-neck colours are reminiscent of English country tweeds. In both versions the background colour changes throughout the garment.*

# Patches

Patches are a wonderful vehicle for using rich groupings of colour. I seem to use two distinctly different approaches to patches, filling them either with plain colour and texture, or with a combination of detailed patterns. You can experiment with colours for the first approach simply by arranging balls of yarn together. For the second try cutting out and arranging patterned fabrics or papers.

## Brick Patches

Brick and stone walls are excellent inspirations for shadings of subtle tones. They are easy to knit being based on regular arrangements of squares and rectangles. I always use as many tones as possible, so, of course, they are best worked in intarsia. As for colours, the variations are endless with hardly two walls alike. For instance, on the right you can see a stack of rich golden London bricks and, in contrast, the glowing pastels of a Maltese wall. A different wall again was the inspiration for the Stone Patch Jacket, page 124.

## Striped Patches

For these patches I often use the 'overlapping from the bottom up' method whereby all the patches start at their lower edges and are 'overlapped' at the top edges as new patches are begun. I find this enables me to knit the patch design off the top of my head, making it up as I go along. The rule for this version is never to allow the top of each patch to show. It should always be interrupted by the next two or three patches. The Striped-patch pullover really came from seeing many striped shirting and linen fabrics together—all those variations on the simple theme of two- and three-colour stripes. The shawl was designed to be in Designers Guild's London shop to go with strongly striped fabrics. I just took all their colourways and my basic triangular shawl pattern (page 15) and came up with the ultimate in overlapping stripes. The coat is another flight of fancy for the Carpet Coat shape (page 42). Follow the shaping instructions but improvise great overlapping patches of vertical and horizontal stripes. I've chosen a dark tweedy palette—rich blues, purples and mossy tweeds strongly accented by wide black stripes.

The yarns I used were chunky tweeds, mohair run with wool and some man-made mixtures and bouclés.

## Woven Patches

This is another of my favourite types of patch design, sending streamers of colour across a garment from all directions. The structure has its own momentum, making the task of choosing colours fairly painless. Unlike many of my patterns where colour choices are continually having to be made, in the Lattice and Ribbon designs (pages 110–21), once you have chosen basic colour groups, the structure takes over.

*You can see opposite the merging of these distinct worlds of colour: the Striped-patch Pullover and Shawl echoing deckchairs in a park; the London bricks (far right) gave birth to the Little Squares Sweater (top centre) seen with my knitted map bedspread; the Ribbon Shawl (below left) is a detail from the one on page 119; the Striped-patch Coat (below right) against my painted cloudscape.*

# Stone Patch

The muted weathered colours of stone walls are a constant inspiration for my work. This is just one example; you can see others on page 122.

## Jacket

The warm creams and greys in this jacket come from a favourite wall I often used to pass in Hampstead in London—strangely formal blocks of white, grey and pinky granite. I added a warm lavender to these colours and surrounded them with a grey-green tweedy yarn. The solid patch colours are livened by lots of texture.

MATERIALS
**Yarns used**
400g (15oz) Rowan Yarns Chunky Tweed in forget-me-not 706 (A); 75g (3oz) in pale pastel 709 (B)
100g (4oz) Rowan Yarns British Wool in fawn cheviot 425 (C)
150g (6oz) Rowan Yarns Light Tweed each in champagne 202 (D) and silver 208 (E); 100g (4oz) in grey 209 (F); 75g (3oz) in scoured 201 (G); 50g (2oz) in rosemix 215 (H)
75g (3oz) Rowan Yarns Fine Cotton Chenille in bran 381 (M); 50g (2oz) each in shark 378 (J) and mole 380 (N); 25g (1oz) in carnation 389 (L)
75g (3oz) Rowan Yarns Double Knitting Wool in pale grey 59 (R); 25g (1oz) each in pinkish cream 84 (Q) and cream 2 (S)
**Equivalent yarn** chunky
1 pair each 5mm (US 8) and 6mm (US 10) needles
8 buttons

(Far right) *This grey and beige colourway is the one specified in the pattern. The Striped Patch Pullover is another overlapping patch design (see also page 122). The red colouring (below) came about when I found all these watermelon pinks, rusts and deep rose tones in a single yarn shop and they cried out to be used together. The tweedy brown base brings out the warm rosiness of the scheme.*

## Squares & Patches

### NOTE
*The finer yarns are used in combination. For example, 'QDE' means one strand each of yarns Q, D and E; 'JJ' means two strands of yarn J. If preferred chunky yarns used singly can be substituted for the combined yarns throughout.*

### TENSION
15 sts and 20 rows to 10cm (4in) over patt on 6mm (US 10) needles.

### MEASUREMENTS
**To fit bust/chest** up to 106cm (42in)
**Actual width** 124cm (49in)
**Length to shoulder** 71cm (28in)
**Side seam** 43cm (17in)
**Sleeve seam** 36cm (14in)

### BACK AND FRONTS (one piece)
Using 5mm (US 8) needles and yarn A, cast on 76 sts.
Work 10 rows K1, P1 rib.
**Next row** Rib 2, K up loop between last st and next st to make 1, (rib 4, make 1) 18 times, rib 1, make 1, rib 1. 96 sts.
Change to 6mm (US 10) needles and work 14 rows st st, beg with a K row (mark each end of last row for pockets).
Commence colour patt from chart, working in st st throughout and twisting yarns between colours to avoid holes, as foll:
**1st row** (rs) K40A, 14C, 42A.
**2nd row** P42A, 14C, 40A.
Cont in patt as set, working colours as indicated on chart itself, until 116 rows in all have been worked from chart, thus ending with a ws row (mark each end of 34th row for pockets).
**Divide for neck and fronts**
**Next row** Patt 44 sts, turn, leaving rem sts on a spare needle and cont on these sts only for right side of neck.
Cast off 4 sts at beg of next row. Work 1 row (this point marks the shoulder line). Dec 1 st at neck edge on next row. 39 sts.
Work 7 rows straight.
**Shape front neck**
Inc 1 st at neck edge on next and foll 2 alt rows. 42 sts. Work 1 row.
Now cast on 2 sts at beg of next row and 4 sts at beg of foll alt row. 48 sts.
Cont as set reversing chart patt from shoulder line, until right front matches back to 1st row of chart, thus ending with a P row (marking equivalent rows on side edge for pockets).
Using yarn A, work 14 rows st st beg with a K row.
Change to 5mm (US 8) needles and work in K1, P1 rib as foll:
**Next row** (K1, P1) twice, (K2 tog, P1, K1, P2 tog, K1, P1) to last 4 sts, K2 tog, P1, K1. 37 sts.
Work 12 rows K1, P1 rib.
Cast off.
With rs facing rejoin yarn to neck edge, cast off 8 sts, patt to end. 44 sts.
Work 1 row. Cast off 4 sts at beg of next row (this point marks the shoulder line). Dec 1 st at neck edge on foll alt row.
Work 5 rows straight. Complete left front to match right.

### SLEEVES
Using 5mm (US 8) needles and yarn A, cast on 32 sts.
Work 10 rows K1, P1 rib.
Change to 6mm (US 10) needles and work 6 rows in st st beg with a K row, inc 1 st at each end of 3rd and 5th rows. 36 sts.
Cont in st st, commence colour patt from chart working between sleeve markers, *at the same time* cont to inc 1 at each end of next and every alt row working the inc sts into patt, as foll:
**1st row** (rs) Inc 1A knitwise, K9A, 14C, 11A, inc 1A knitwise. 38 sts.
**2nd row** P13A, 14C, 11A.
Cont as set until 51 rows in all have been worked from chart. 88 sts.
Work 5 rows straight.
Cast off.

### POCKET LININGS AND EDGINGS
Using 6mm (US 10) needles for linings and 5mm (US 8) for edgings and yarn A, work as given for Zigzag Jacket on page 63.

### BUTTON BAND
Using 5mm (US 8) needles and yarn A, with rs facing K up 104 sts along right front edge (for a man's jacket, left front edge for a woman's jacket).
P 1 row. K 2 rows to form foldline.
Change to yarns REF and work 9 rows st st, beg with a K row.
Cast off.

### BUTTONHOLE BAND
Using 5mm (US 8) needles and yarn A, with rs facing K up 104 sts along left front edge (for a man's jacket, right front edge for a woman's), *at the same time* make buttonholes on K up row as foll:
**K up and buttonhole row** K up 2 sts, (K up 2 sts, lift 2nd st on right-hand needle over 1st st and off needle, K up 1 st, lift 2nd st on right-hand needle over 1st st and off, K up 11) 8 times, ending last rep K up 1.
**Next row** P to end casting on 2 sts over those cast off in previous row.
K 2 rows to form foldline.
Change to yarns REF.
**Next row** K2, (cast off 2 sts, K12 including st used to cast off) 8 times ending last rep K2.
**Next row** P to end casting on 2 sts over those cast off in previous row.
Work 7 rows st st beg with a K row.
Cast off.

### TO MAKE UP
Fold front bands on to ws and catch down.
**Collar**
Using 5mm (US 8) needles and yarn A, with rs facing K up 65 sts evenly around neck edge.
Work 9 rows K1, P1 rib.
Cast off in rib.
Fold pocket edgings on to ws and catch down.
Set sleeves in flat, matching centre of cast-off edge to shoulder line.
Join side and sleeve seams.
Catch down pocket linings on to ws of fronts.
Neaten buttonholes. Sew on buttons.

# Stone Patch

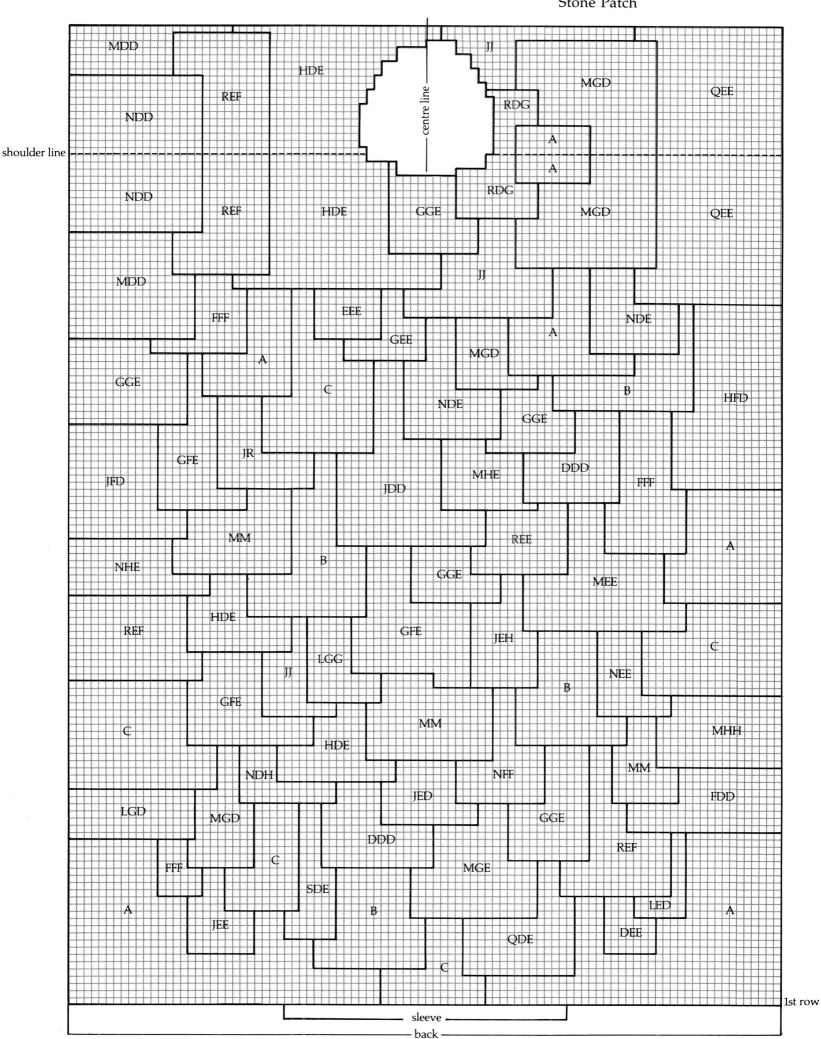

shoulder line

centre line

1st row

sleeve

back

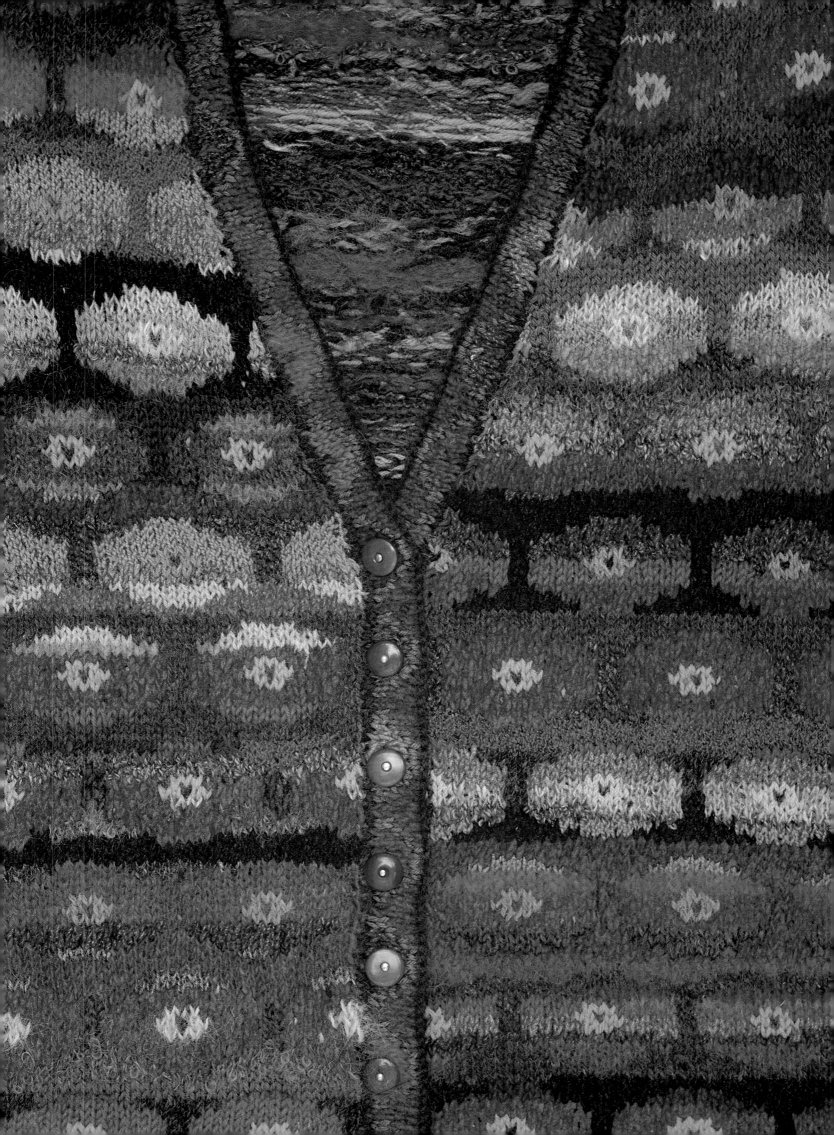

# CIRCLES

After the angular corners of squares we move on to the sumptuous curves of circles. When I first became interested in knitting and canvaswork I was told by experts in my local yarn shop, 'You cannot make circles in knitting or canvaswork,' with much the same severity that people used to say, 'Redheads should never wear green.' I can't resist challenges like that and immediately launched into a series of circles in canvaswork—my first millefiori paperweight design. The deliciously playful rings of small circles contained within a larger circle was irresistible, and the success of this taught me my first lesson about design—when in doubt, try it!

The circle is such a basic form that even crude distortions of it are easily comprehended. The very world is a circle among circles. The eye is a wonderful series of circles and through our circular lenses we view the world. So it's not surprising that circular shapes are very comforting and satisfying to us.

For some quick experiments with circular designs try arranging objects that suggest circles on different coloured backgrounds. You could use flowers, for instance, or cut fruit and vegetables or beads or buttons (you can see what I mean on the next two pages). Alternatively, cut circles out of coloured paper. Your arrangements can be random or precisely laid out in a staggered or grid-like pattern. Moving the objects apart gives the arrangement a floaty feeling. Placing them close together creates a rich dense texture. When playing like this it is important to look hard at the results. It's best if you do your arrangements on the floor so that you can see them from a distance by standing on a chair above them.

Once you start thinking about circles, you will begin seeing them everywhere—in greengrocers' shops in pyramids of circular fruit, in iron manhole covers on the street, in flower pots in a garden nursery, and on many of the dress and shirt prints walking about.

Look for unexpected or pleasing arrangements of colours to use in yarn experiments. Once you can see an idea laid out roughly you will have the courage to plough ahead holding the idea in your mind's eye through the inevitable awkward stages of any creation. Even the most brilliant and professional garments can look like 'nothing on earth' while they are growing, and many would-be designers crumble at the half-way stage because they don't know how to judge a particular composition or find it hard to visualize the end product. Colours can look too bright or too dull; half-finished circles can look too tall or too flat. It can all get very harrowing! So we all need courage to soldier on and that can come from having seen a group of colours or motifs in some other form, and been struck by the 'rightness of it all'. This is why designers are always looking at all the bits of colour and pattern around them to experience the effects of those unexpected arrangements.

*(Far left) The dark version of the Persian Poppy Waistcoat (page 140) was designed for a New York lady who liked the chic of the dark background and the punch of the reds and brilliant blues. I found the old maroon buttons in a market. Notice the amount of colour in the band.*

*(Overleaf) A few of the endless possibilities of arrangements of circles using buttons, bowls, cut fruits, spools of yarn, succulents in pots, fruit tarts, beads, paperweights and flower heads. You can also see four versions of Persian Poppy, two of Floating Circles, one of Little Circles, and also my earliest experiments with circles, the Red Jacket (see also page 156) and Steve's Jacket (made for Steve Lovi).*

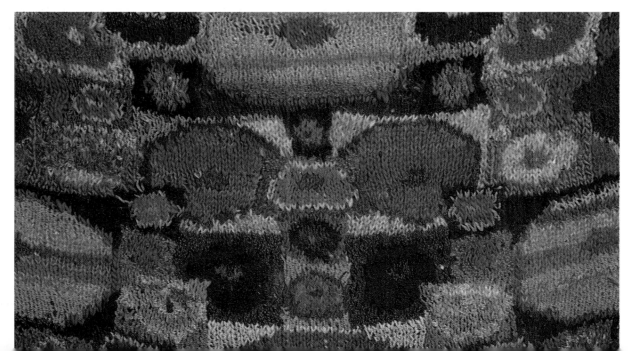

*(Left) A section of one of my shawls. Like the Squares Shawl on page 107, it plays with various different scales of a motif, in this case circles in squares. I've used a rich, jewel-like palette but more subtle schemes could be employed.*

Circles

# Floating Circles

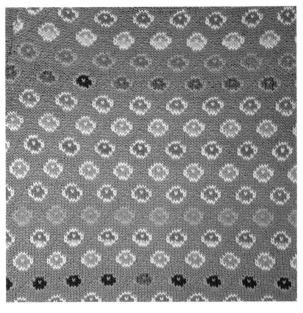

The pattern for this crew-neck sweater consists of rows of circles on a plain background, with a fifteen-row border at the cuffs and waist and a narrower one round the neck. I chose the sweet pea colours given in the pattern as a contrast to the black version (which I'd done earlier). The main colour was a grass green to start with but I changed it to this soft sage which gives a glowing background to the sprightly pastels.

You will notice the odd circle in different tones from the rest of its row. I Swiss-darned these on afterwards to break up the insistent row-by-row effect and make the eye move all over the pattern. Some two- and three-colour designs can get very 'stripey', making the eye go to and fro as at a tennis match.

The sweater is knitted entirely in wool but you could try fine cotton chenille, mohair or tapestry yarn—anything as long as it can be knitted up to the correct tension. The design changes dramatically according to the colours used. Even adjusting the colours given in the pattern would result in a totally different mood. Imagine using pink as the background instead of sage green. Or try something quite different—all reds, perhaps, or forest greens, turquoise and rusts. I find it helps to keep the outline colours lighter than the background (like a halo of light round each circle).

## MATERIALS
**Yarn used**
300[300,325]g (11[11,12]oz) Rowan Yarns Double Knitting Wool in sage green 417 (A); 100[100,125]g (4[4,5]oz) in ivory 1 (G); 50g (2oz) each in salmon pink 66 (B), mauve 92 (C), pale blue 48 (H), bright pink 95 (J) and purple 611 (L); 25g (1oz) each in light maroon 70 (D), apricot 20 (E), pale purple 127 (F), lavender 121 (M), rose pink 19 (N), deep peach 21 (Q) and pink 68 (R)
**Equivalent yarn** double knitting
1 pair each 3¼mm (US 3) and 4mm (US 6) needles

## TENSION
24 sts and 25 rows to 10cm (4in) over patt on 4mm (US 6) needles.

## MEASUREMENTS
**To fit bust/chest** 91[96,101]cm (36[38,40]in)
**Actual width at underarm** 98[106,114]cm (38½[41½,45]in)
**Length to shoulder** 58[61,64]cm 22½[24,25]in)
**Side seam** 34[37,39]cm (13½[14½,15½]in)
**Sleeve seam** 38[40,42]cm (15[16,16½]in)

## BACK
Using 3¼mm (US 3) needles and yarn B, cast on 95[105,115] sts.
Work 9 rows st st, beg with a K row.
**Next row** K to end to form hemline.
Change to 4mm (US 6) needles and yarn C, and commence colour patt from chart as foll:
Beg with a K row work in st st, inc 1 st at each end of 11th row and every foll 7th[8th,8th] row until there are 117[127,137] sts, *at the same time* work contrast colours as shown in colour sequence table (weave yarns into back of work where they are carried over more than 5 sts and work inc sts into patt).

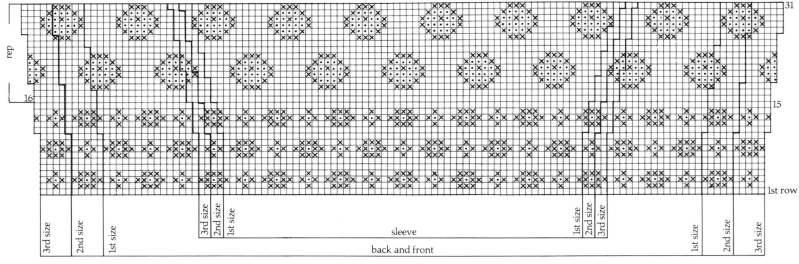

**Key**   □ = main colour   ⊠ = 1st contrast colour   ⊡ = 2nd contrast colour   **Note:** *see colour sequence table for actual colours*

When 31 rows have been worked from chart, work 16th–31st rows again. These 16 rows form the patt rep.

Cont in patt until 86[92,98] rows have been worked after hemline row.

**Shape armholes**

Keeping patt correct, cast off 6 sts at beg of next 2 rows, then 2 sts at beg of foll 4 rows.

Now dec 1 st at each end of foll 4[5,6] alt rows. 89[97,105] sts.

Cont in patt until 144[152,160] rows have been worked after hemline row, thus ending with a P row.

**Shape shoulders and back neck**

Cast off 8[9,10] sts, patt 23[26,29] sts, cast off 27 sts, patt to end.

**Next row** Cast off 8[9,10] sts, patt to neck edge, turn, leaving rem sts on a spare needle, cont on these sts only for left side of neck. 23[26,29] sts.

**Next row** Cast off 6 sts, patt to end.

**Next row** Cast off 7[9,10] sts, patt to neck edge. 10[11,13] sts.

**Next row** Cast off 3 sts, patt to end.

Cast off rem 7[8,10] sts.

With ws facing rejoin yarn to neck edge and complete right side to match left.

## FRONT

Work as for back until 120[128,136] rows have been worked after hemline row, thus ending with a P row.

**Shape neck**

**Next row** Patt 37[41,45] sts, cast off 15 sts, patt to end.

**Next row** Patt to neck edge, turn, leaving rem sts on a spare needle, cont on these sts only for right side of neck. 37[41,45] sts.

Cast off 3 sts at neck edge on next row, then 2 sts on 2 foll alt rows. Now dec 1 st at neck edge on 8 foll alt rows. 22[26,30] sts.

Work 2 rows straight.

**Shape shoulder**

Cast off 8[9,10] sts at beg of next row and 7[9,10] sts at beg of foll alt row.

Work 1 row.

Cast off rem 7[8,10] sts.

With ws facing rejoin yarn to neck edge and complete left side to match right.

## SLEEVES

Using 3¼mm (US 3) needles and yarn B, cast on 57[61,65] sts.

Work as given for back until 15 rows of border have been worked after hemline row, foll chart between sleeve markers and inc 1 st at each end of 11th chart row. 59[63,67] sts.

Now work circle patt from chart, inc 1 st at each end of next and every foll 4th[5th,5th] row until there are 93[97,101] sts, *at the same time*, for the first 8 rows, foll colour sequence as given for 136th–143rd rows of back, then foll colour sequence as for 16th row of back to end.

Cont in patt until 94[100,106] rows in all have been worked after hemline row, ending on same patt row as back at armhole.

**Shape top**

Keeping patt correct, cast off 6 sts at beg of next 2 rows, then 2 sts at beg of foll 4 rows. 73[77,81] sts.

Dec 1 st at each end of next 10[12,13] alt rows and then every foll row until there are 37[37,39] sts on needle. Now cast off 3 sts at the beg of the foll 6 rows. 19[19,21] sts.

Cast off.

## TO MAKE UP

Join left shoulder seam.

**Neckband**

Using 4mm (US 6) needles and yarn A, with rs facing K up 46 sts evenly across back neck and 75 sts around front neck. 121 sts.

**1st row** (ws) P to end in H.

**2nd row** *K1H, 3J, 3H, 1J, 2H; rep from * to last st, 1H.

**3rd row** *P1J, 1H, 1J, 1D, 1J, 1H, 2J, 1D, 1J; rep from * to last st, 1J.

**4th row** As 2nd row.

**5th row** As 1st row.

Change to 3¼mm (US 3) needles and yarn B.

K 3 rows to form foldline.

Work 7 rows st st, beg with a P row.

Cast off very loosely to allow hem to stretch round curve.

Join right shoulder seam. Join armhole seams. Join side and sleeve seams.

Fold hems on to ws and catch down.

Swiss-darn three or four circles at random in different tones to those used in the rest of the row to which they belong.

(Above) *Something about this Black Circles colourway reminds me of Russian ballet costumes. Maybe it's the jewel-like reds and purples against the black ground, or perhaps the detailed borders. It's photographed against my red mural.*

(Overleaf) *Both versions of the Floating Circles Crew-neck Sweater in Kew Gardens in spring.*

| COLOUR SEQUENCE TABLE | | | | | | | |
|---|---|---|---|---|---|---|---|
| **rows** | ☐ | ☒ | ⚫ | **rows** | ☐ | ☒ | ⚫ |
| 1–5 | C | D | E | 84–87 | A | G | M |
| 6–10 | F | A | G | 88–91 | A | G | C |
| 11–15 | H | J | D | 92–95 | A | G | B |
| 16–23 | A | G | L | 96–103 | A | H | J |
| 24–31 | A | M | D | 104–111 | A | H | L |
| 32–35 | A | G | C | 112–116 | A | G | R |
| 36–39 | A | G | M | 117–119 | A | G | N |
| 40–43 | A | G | E | 120–127 | A | G | J |
| 44–47 | A | G | J | 128–135 | A | G | F |
| 48–55 | A | H | Q | 136–140 | A | G | E |
| 56–63 | A | G | F | 141–143 | A | G | Q |
| 64–69 | A | G | C | 144–147 | A | G | C |
| 70–71 | A | G | M | 148–151 | A | G | B |
| 72–79 | A | G | J | 152–155 | A | G | H |
| 80–83 | A | G | H | 156–161 | A | G | M |

# Little Circles

The first version of this was intended for a man and the overall look of it was quite tweedy. Since then I have tried this pattern in many different schemes. The latest is this bright number in oriental yellows and high pastels. Alternatively, try the softer silvery colourway on page 138, which uses all the sugared almond colours (these are particularly flattering to anyone with a pale, delicate complexion).

The yarn is all double knitting wool. If you want to get more texture into the pattern you could use a combination of fine tweeds, chenilles and wool, although personally I feel that the pattern creates a visual texture of its own.

When you are working with three colours to a row, as here, it is important to knit with a relaxed even tension. The colours being carried across the back must not be pulled too tightly or the result will be a long thin garment. If you do find that your work is puckering, try exaggerating the looseness of the yarns being stranded across the back. If you find you are an incorrigibly tight knitter, give this design a miss—or give to a loose-knitting friend to do it for you!

## Yellow Pullover

### MATERIALS
**Yarn used**
125[125,150]g (5[5,6]oz) Rowan Yarns Double Knitting Wool in mustard 8 (A); 50[50,75]g (2[2,3]oz) in lavender 121 (G); 50g (2oz) each in lime green 76 (F) and khaki 105 (C); 25[25,50]g (1[1,2]oz) each in pinky lavender 128 (B) and deep peach 21 (D); 25g (1oz) each in apricot 20 (E), raspberry 93 (H), deep pink 96 (J), forget-me-not 123 (L), primrose 6 (M), canary yellow 12 (N) and pink 68 (Q)
**Equivalent yarn** double knitting
1 pair each 3¾mm (US 5) and 4½mm (US 7) needles

### TENSION
24 sts and 21 rows to 10cm (4in) over patt on 4½mm (US 7) needles.

### MEASUREMENTS
**To fit bust/chest** 86[91,96]cm (34[36,38]in)
**Actual width** 94[101,108]cm (37[40,42½]in)
**Length to shoulder** 60cm (23½in)
**Side seam** 37cm (14½in)

### BACK
Using 3¾mm (US 5) needles and yarn B, cast on 88[96,104] sts.
Work in K1, P1 rib as foll: 1 row in C, 2 rows in D, 2 rows in E, 4 rows in A, 1 row in E, 1 row in F, 6 rows in A.
**Next row** With A, rib 8[12,4], K up loop between last st and next st to make 1, (rib 3[3,4], make 1) 24 times, rib 8[12,4]. 113[121,129] sts.
Change to 4½mm (US 7) needles and commence colour patt from chart, working in st st throughout and stranding contrast yarns across the back of the work, as foll:

**1st row** (rs) K2G, *5A, 3G; rep from * to last 7 sts, 5A, 2G.
**2nd row** P2H, 1G, 3A, 1G, *3H, 1G, 3A, 1G; rep from * to last 2 sts, 2H.
Cont in patt as set, rep 2nd–11th rows on chart until 68 rows have been completed and foll colour sequence table for colour changes.**
**Shape armholes**
Cast off 6 sts at beg of next 2 rows, then 2 sts at beg of foll 4 rows. 93[101,109] sts.
Now dec 1 st at each end of every alt row until 81[89,97] sts rem.
Cont in patt without shaping until 112[116,120] patt rows have been worked.

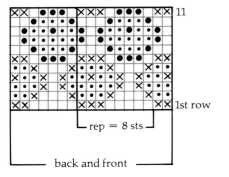

rep = 8 sts

back and front

### COLOUR SEQUENCE TABLE
Work the circle motifs from the chart using different colours for each band of motifs as follows (the outline colour ● or ⊠ on the chart is given first, and then the inner colour, · on the chart):

| motif band | yellow | | silver | |
|---|---|---|---|---|
| | ● or ⊠ | · | ● or ⊠ | · |
| 1 | G | H | G | H |
| 2 | G | J | D | G |
| 3 | L | C | J | D |
| 4 | C | B | D | B |
| 5 | M | G | E | D |
| 6 | G | M | C | E |
| 7 | H | G | H | C |
| 8 | G | D | G | D |
| 9 | F | G | L | E |
| 10 | N | D | E | F |
| 11 | C | N | F | D |
| 12 | Q | H | D | L |
| 13 | Q | D | D | B |
| 14 | F | G | C | J |
| 15 | H | F | G | H |
| 16 | F | B | G | J |
| 17 | G | N | J | L |
| 18 | D | Q | L | C |
| 19 | H | F | E | B |
| 20 | J | B | H | E |
| 21 | M | L | E | F |
| 22 | F | C | F | G |
| 23 | C | M | G | L |
| 24 | G | E | H | G |
| 25 | F | G | D | B |

(Far right) *The yellow version of Little Circles was directly inspired by the colours of oriental silk brocades. The Persian Poppy Shawl (page 143) is thrown over the basket in the background.*

*We spotted this little circular mosaic on a building in Gozo. The washes of bright pastels could be a superb colouring for a garment.*

*(Far right) On the left is the original tweedy colour colouring for the Little Circles Pullover contrasting nicely with the silvery mother-of-pearl colours given in the pattern. Photographed at Hidcote Manor in Gloucestershire among the Japanese anemones.*

**Shape shoulders**
Cast off 6[8,10] sts at beg of next 2 rows then 7[8,9] sts at beg of next 4 rows. Leave rem 41 sts on a spare needle.

FRONT
Work as given for back to **.
**Shape armholes and divide for neck**
**Next row** Cast off 8 sts, patt 48[52,56] sts including st used to cast off, turn, leaving rem sts on a spare needle and cont on these sts only for left side of neck. Dec 1 st at neck edge on next and foll 15 alt rows, then on 4 foll 3rd rows, *at the same time* cast off 2 sts at armhole edge on next 2 alt rows and 1 st on foll 4 alt rows. 20[24,28] sts.
Cont in patt until front matches back to shoulder shaping ending at armhole edge.
**Shape shoulder**
Cast off 6[8,10] sts at beg of next row and 7[8,9] sts at beg of foll alt row.
Work 1 row. Cast off rem 7[8,9] sts.
Rejoin yarn to sts on spare needle at centre front.
**Next row** K2 tog, patt to end.
**Next row** Cast off 8 sts, patt to neck edge. 48[52,56] sts.
Complete to match left side, reversing shapings.

TO MAKE UP
Backstitch left shoulder seam.
**Neckband**
Using 3¾mm (US 5) needles and yarn A, with rs facing K across 41 sts of back neck, 49[53,57] sts down left front neck and 49[53,57] sts up right front neck. 139[147,155] sts.
Work in K1, P1 rib as foll:
**1st row** Rib 47[51,55], P2 tog, P2 tog tbl, rib to end.
**2nd row** With E, rib 87[91,95], K2 tog tbl, K2 tog, rib to end.
**3rd row** With E, rib 45[49,53], P2 tog, P2 tog tbl, rib to end.
Cont to dec at front neck in this way working knitwise decs on rs rows and purlwise decs on ws rows in colours as foll: 4th–5th rows in D, 6th row in C, 7th row in B.
Cast off in B, dec as before.

Backstitch right shoulder seam.
**Armbands**
Using 3¾mm (US 5) needles and yarn A, with rs facing K up 104[112,120] sts evenly around armhole edge.
**1st row** P to end in B.
**2nd–3rd rows** K to end in C.
**4th–7th rows** Work in st st in A, beg with a K row.
Cast off loosely.
Backstitch side seams.
Fold under armhole edges and catch down lightly.

## Silver Pullover

MATERIALS
**Yarn used**
125[125,150]g (5[5,6]oz) Rowan Yarns Double Knitting Wool in silver blue 64 (A); 50[75,75]g (2[3,3]oz) in fawn 82 (F); 50[50,75]g (2[2,3]oz) each in peach 79 (D), ivory 1 (E) and lemon 4 (G); 25[25,50]g (1[1,2]oz) each in deep peach 22 (C), pink 68 (H) and pinky lavender 128 (J); 25g (1oz) each in sky blue 123 (B) and acid green 32 (L)
**Equivalent yarn** double knitting
1 pair each 3¾mm (US 5) and 4½mm (US 7) needles

TO MAKE
The tension and measurements are the same as for the yellow colourway.
The instructions are also the same, with the following exceptions.
**Back and front**
Substitute foll colours for ribs: 2 rows A, 1 row H, 1 row F, 1 row A, 1 row C, 3 rows D, 1 row A, 1 row J, 1 row B, 1 row A, 1 row F, 1 row H.
**Neckband**
Substitute the foll colours: K up and 1 row A, 1 row L, 1 row J, 1 row A, 2 rows D, 1 row C.
Cast off in A.
**Armbands**
Work in K1, P1 rib: 1 row A, 1 row H, 1 row J, 1 row A. Cast off in D.

# Persian Poppy

This design is a delicious cheat. Although it has a rich display of colour changes, it is effectively knitted as a two-colour design for the most part—the poppy centres being a third colour every ten rows or so. I invented the waistcoat design for Beatrice Bellini (owner of a long established knitwear shop in London) so that she could give her knitters the same simple instructions yet never end up with two garments alike.

*The neutral background of the waistcoat gives a quiet base for the cool lemons and lavenders of the poppies. This light on dark scheme is reversed in the pullover with its light ground and deep rust and gunmetal poppies. You could try this colouring on the waistcoat or any two-colours-a-row pattern. It's also exciting to change scale, as I did in the pullover, simply by using larger needles and thicker yarn.*

What you do is this: take at least a dozen colours for your background and another dozen or so for your 'poppies', choosing fairly close tones for the poppies and a more varied selection for the background (again close tones, but with some surprises—if earthy colours, add some sky blue and pale green 'lighteners'). First, place the poppy colours around your chair. Take the first colour; and break off about an arm's length of it and wind it into a small ball. Break off a length of the second colour and continue winding the ball with that, tying it to the first colour with a simple knot and leaving 5cm (2in) ends on both. Then take a third colour and tie that on, and so on through the poppy colours, winding on a slightly different length every time, until you have a ball about the size of a tennis ball. Do the same with the background colours.

The only rule I use is to go from one colour to the nearest in value to it, working, say, from darkest grey to medium to light, and on to sky blue or whatever. Sometimes you might like great jumps in contrast so experiment with many different colours and textures. The design is greatly enhanced by changes of texture: mix in chenille, mohair, silk, bouclé, and so on, or twist thin yarns together to make up the approximate average weight of the yarn being used.

After you have made up your two tennis balls of background and poppy colours, knit a row of poppies and see if you are enjoying the colours and the spacing of the yarn lengths. It will probably be a little difficult to tell at this stage, but at least you'll be able to see if the poppies are 'reading' against the background, or if there are any shrieking colours that should be left out.

For the poppy centres I usually choose a rich, singing tone and I try to keep the colour the same for each row of poppies, though it does vary from one row of poppies to another. By the way, the long tails at each join should be knitted in at the back of the work as you go along.

Once you've tried this method on the Persian Poppy Waistcoat or Shawl, you'll certainly want to adapt it to something else. Many basic two- or three-colour repeating patterns can be worked in this way.

## Waistcoat

This design will really throw you in at the deep end. I can tell you exactly what yarns I used, but in no way can you be told how much of each colour to use or exactly where to put it. In fact, it's the ideal design for using up oddments and leftovers.

However, if you want a garment similar to the one here, buy one ball each of all the yarns listed. I used 29 different colours in double knitting wool, fine tweeds and cottons in a range of butter yellows, lavenders and pale light pinks for the poppies and silver grey, sky blues, mint greens, tweedy lavender and deeper greys for the background. Several bright pinks and magentas are used for the centre dots. You will definitely have lots of yarn left over but these can be added to your stockpile and need not be wasted.

MATERIALS

**Yarn used**

**Edgings** (A) 50g (2oz) Rowan Yarns Light Tweed in grey 209

**Background colours** (B) 25g (1oz) Rowan Yarns Double Knitting Wool each in pale grey 59, pale pink 109 and fawn 82; Fine Cotton Chenille in shark 378; Light Tweed in grey 209, silver 208, scoured 201 and rosemix 215; Handknit Cotton in sky blue 264, lilac 269 and mint 270

**Poppy colours** (C) 25g (1oz) each in Double Knitting Wool in cream/yellow 7, peach 79, lemon 4, sponge 402 and cream 2; Fine Cotton Chenille in bran 381 and carnation 389; Light Tweed in champagne 202, rosemix 215,

bamboo 218 and scoured 201; Handknit Cotton in flesh 268, lemon 265 and sky blue 264
**Poppy centres** (D) 25g (1oz) each in Double Knitting Wool in bright pink 95 and mid pink 69; Light Tweed in lavender 213
**Equivalent yarn** double knitting
1 pair each 3¼mm (US 3) and 4mm (US 6) needles
6 buttons

## NOTE
*Prepare yarns as described above.*

## TENSION
27 sts and 27 rows to 10cm (4in) over patt on 4mm (US 6) needles.

## MEASUREMENTS
**To fit bust/chest** 86[91,96]cm (34[36,38]in)
**Actual width** 91[96,100]cm (36[38,39½]in)
**Length to shoulder** 56[58,59]cm (22[23,23½]in)
**Side seam** 30[32,33]cm (12[12½,13]in)

## BACK
Using 3¼mm (US 3) needles and yarn A, cast on 123[129,135] sts.
Work 9 rows st st beg with a K row.
K 1 row to form hemline. Beg with a K row, work 2 rows st st.
Change to 4mm (US 6) needles and yarn B and commence colour patt from chart 1, working between back markers and weaving yarns into back of work when not in use.
**1st row** (rs) K.
**2nd row** P.
**3rd row** K2B[5B,(2C,6B)], *6B, 5C, 6B; rep from * to last 2[5,8] sts, 2B[5B,(6B,2C)].
**4th row** P2B[(1C,4B),(4C,4B)], *4B, 9C, 4B; rep from * to last 2[5,8] sts, 2B[(4B,1C),(4B,4C)].
Cont in patt as set, rep 1st–26th rows of chart until work measures 31[32,33]cm (12[12½,13]in) from hemline row, ending with a ws row.
**Shape armholes**
Cast off 5[6,7] sts at beg of next 2 rows. Now dec 1 st at each end of next 6 rows and on foll 8[9,10] alt rows. 85[87,89] sts.
Cont in patt without shaping until work measures 56[58,59]cm (22[22½,23]in), ending with a ws row.
**Shape shoulders and divide for neck**
Cast off 6 sts at beg of next 2 rows.
**Next row** Cast off 6 sts, patt 21 sts including st used to cast off, cast off 19[21,23] sts, patt to end.
**Next row** Cast off 6 sts, patt to neck edge, turn, leaving rem sts on a spare needle, and cont on these sts only for left side of neck. 21 sts.
Cast off 4 sts at beg of next row, then 6 sts at beg of foll row and 4 sts at beg of foll row.
Cast off rem 7 sts.
With ws facing, rejoin yarn to sts on spare needle at neck edge and complete to match left side reversing shapings.

## LEFT FRONT
Using 3¼mm (US 3) needles and yarn A, cast on 62[65,68] sts.
Work 9 rows st st beg with a K row.
K 1 row to form hemline. Beg with a K row, work 2 rows st st.
Change to 4mm (US 6) needles and yarn B and

commence colour patt from chart 2, working between left front markers.
Cont in patt until work measures 7[11,13] rows less than back to armhole shaping, ending at front edge.
**Shape neck and armholes**
Dec 1 st at neck edge on next and every foll 4th row, *at the same time* when work measures 31[32,33]cm (12[12½,13]in) shape armhole by casting off 5[6,7] sts at armhole edge on next row, then dec 1 st at armhole edge on next row and on foll 8[9,10] alt rows.
Cont to dec at neck edge as before until 35[34,34] sts rem, then dec 1 st at neck edge on every foll 3rd row until 25 sts rem.
Cont without shaping until work matches back to shoulder, ending at armhole edge.
**Shape shoulder**
Cast off 6 sts at beg of next 3 alt rows.
Work 1 row.
Cast off rem 7 sts.

**Chart 1**

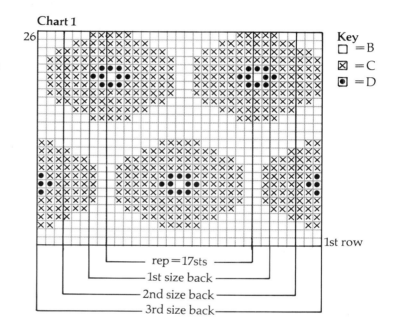

Key
□ = B
☒ = C
⊙ = D

rep = 17sts
1st size back
2nd size back
3rd size back

**Chart 2**

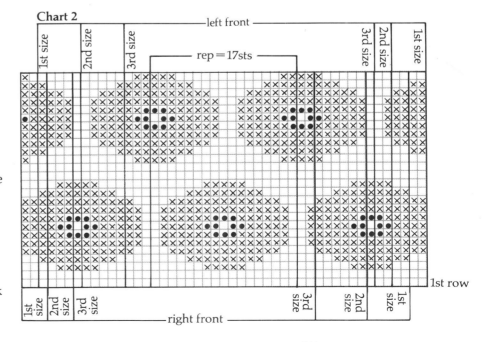

## Circles

**Chart 3**

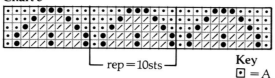

└─ rep = 10sts ─┘

**Key**
⊡ = A

### RIGHT FRONT
Work as given for left front, working between right front markers on chart 2 and reversing all shapings.

### TO MAKE UP
Join shoulder seams.
**Armbands**
Using 3¼mm (US 3) needles and yarn A, with rs of work facing, K up 108 sts around armhole edge. P 1 row.
K 3 rows to form foldline.
Work 3 rows st st beg with a P row.
Cast off.
Join side seams. Fold hem on to ws and catch down.
**Front band**
Using 4mm (US 6) needles and yarn A, with rs of work facing and beg at lower right front edge, K up 70 sts to beg of neck shaping, then 72[76,80] sts along shaped front edge, then 37[39,41] sts around back neck, then 72[76,80] sts along shaped left front edge and 70 sts from beg of neck shaping to lower left front edge. 321[331,341] sts.
Commence colour patt from chart 3, using yarn A and any other two chosen contrast colours, working in st st throughout and beg with a P row.
Work 1st and 2nd rows.
**3rd row** Patt 263[273,283] sts, (cast off 2 sts, patt 8 sts including st used to cast off) 5 times, cast off 2 sts, patt to end.
**4th row** Patt to end casting on 2 sts over those cast off in previous row.
**5th row** Patt to end.
Change to 3¼mm (US 3) needles and yarn A. K 2 rows to form foldline.
Work 2 rows st st beg with a K row.
**Next row** K6, (cast off 2 sts, K8 including st used to cast off) 6 times, K to end.
**Next row** P to end, casting on 2 sts over those cast off in previous row.
K 1 row. P 1 row.
Cast off.
Neaten buttonholes. Sew on buttons.

*This was the original version of Persian Poppy. In it I returned yet again to one of my all-time favourite schemes, old faded oriental carpet colours. The shots of sky blue and camel lighten the heavier reds and browns.*

## Shawl

For this shawl I used my basic triangular shawl pattern (see page 15) and, at least to begin with, the same chart as for the Persian Poppy Waistcoat (page 141).

### THE YARNS

I started with a group of coppery to rose tones in mohair, chenille and wool mixtures for the poppies, and a group of warm greys, sludgy greens and camel tones (also in a wide range of textures) for the background.

The yarns were prepared exactly as they were for the waistcoat, by making two balls of varying lengths in each group of colours. However, since the triangle gradually grows wider, you need shorter lengths at the bottom of the shawl. One tends to get lazy about making these balls and put longer and longer lengths of each colour on, which is all right but it does make for large blank areas.

As before, the best way of checking that you have your colours and amounts about right is to make up tennis-ball-sized balls of background and poppy colours and knit up a few rows to see how they look. If too much of a strong colour begins to appear you can always break it off and jump to the next one. Sometimes I like the poppy to have larger areas of a single colour while the background colour changes more rapidly, giving only a row or two of each colour. It's very much a matter of individual taste, and it's hard to do anything wrong with this pattern as long as you

have enough colours to start with—at least twelve in each ball, if not twenty!

### THE POPPIES

After knitting about a third of the shawl with coppery poppies on a lighter background, I started golden poppies on a slightly darker background on each side, letting these poppies get larger and larger, and creating two side triangles hemming in the diamond of the lighter centre.

To make the poppies larger I just start them off with more and more space between each one. So instead of leaving twelve stitches in the background colour between each five stitches of poppy colour, as in the first row of the pattern, you can leave sixteen on the second band of poppies and eighteen on the next one. This gives you enough room for the poppies to get deeper as they expand. If this sounds very imprecise, it's because I always find it best just to feel my way through a design, letting mistakes and mishaps shape the result. I usually head for symmetry but, if I leave out a few stitches between the poppies and have to add more to compensate, I'm delighted. It helps to give that wonderful, human primitive quality I love so much in oriental textiles.

The only rule I try to follow in these designs is to cram everything as tightly together as possible in a lovely cosy jumble of shapes. Often I see designs that look a little 'mean', not filling the space enough. Be bold and varied with your colours and you can't fail as far as I'm concerned.

# FLOWERS

So far we've explored strictly geometric approaches to pattern; now, in complete contrast, we come to flowers—one of the most eternal and universal of themes. Flowers represent freshness, innocence, fragility, regeneration.

From a design point of view, the thousands, maybe millions, of shapes and colours in the world of flowers alone could provide enough food for the imagination to last several lifetimes. Throughout history and in every art or craft tradition all over the world, flower motifs and designs and flower-based patterns have been used in infinitely diverse ways, from the bold simplicity of peasant decoration on furniture and textiles to the richest, most intricate embellishments on china and wall-coverings and in lace and embroidery.

I'm only playing with one flower here—changing scale, arrangement and, above all, colours to give you a taste of the experiments you can make with whatever theme you choose.

(Opposite) *The profusion of flowers is a mere taste of the decorative use of this joyful theme. The bright pastel flowers on a Japanese kimono, an embroidered silk shawl and my Caucasian Flower needlepoint contrast with the cool flat colours of English jugs and wallpaper. The severe black, cream and grey cloisonné vases are another direction as are the explosive reds, blues and white below.*

# Damask Flower

The Damask Flower motif originated in a detail of a beautiful fragment of eighteenth-century Spanish silk damask which I saw in *Textile Collections of the World*. I often pore over such volumes in my constant search for interesting schemes. What caught my eye about this design was the suggestion of roundness and petals in what was nevertheless a simple two-colour design.

When I found the flower, I first sketched it in pencils on graph paper. Then I organized the stitches to make a shape I liked, starting with the right-hand side of the flower and copying it exactly on the left-hand side to create a mirror image. If you do this sort of thing yourself, you can hold a mirror up to the first half to see what it will eventually look like. Being a mirror image makes it much easier to knit—you soon learn the rhythm of the pattern as you finish one flower after another, until you can almost do without the chart by the last flower.

## Peplum Jacket

I used a pale turquoise fine cotton chenille—the same colour throughout—for the flowers. The background is made up of stripes (no more than four rows each) in about ten to fourteen colours in various cotton yarns, but you could use more or fewer colours if you wanted. The main idea is to keep the background as rich and varied as possible with many colour changes. I kept the colours fairly close in tone, but you could use really climactic changes of colour, like those in the original Persian Poppy on page 142.

The flower centres go from pink at the base to pinkish white at the top of the flower. To give a real glow to the centres, knit the first two rows in the deepest colour, then one row in a medium tone and the last two rows much lighter.

*This is Zoë's favourite shape and one that she invented. With its neat fitted body, flared peplum and puffed sleeves, it's probably the most feminine garment in my repertoire. Seen below and on pages 148–49, it looks good with trousers or a full skirt.*

MATERIALS
Approx 200[250]g (8[9]oz) mixed yarns and colours averaging double knitting weight for background colours (A)
Approx 350[400]g (13[15]oz) fine chenille in one colour for flowers (B)
Oddments of mixed yarns for flower centres (C)
1 pair each 3¼mm (US 3) and 4mm (US 6) needles
1 3.00mm (US D/3) crochet hook
8 buttons

TENSION
22 sts and 26 rows to 10cm (4in) over patt on 4mm (US 6) needles.

MEASUREMENTS
**To fit bust** 81–86[86–92]cm (32–34[34–36]in)
**Actual underarm width** 91[94.5]cm (36[37]in)
**Length to shoulder** 53cm (21in) including peplum
**Side seam** 24cm (9½in) excluding peplum
**Sleeve seam** 45cm (17½in)

BACK
Using 4mm (US 6) needles and yarn A, cast on 84[88] sts.
Work in st st, commence colour patt from chart, weaving contrast colours into back of work, as foll:
**1st row** (rs) K 0[2], (5A, 2B, 11A, 2B, 1A, 6B, 1A, 2B, 6A) twice, 5A, 2B, 5[7]A.
**2nd row** P 0[2B] (1B, 3A, 4B, 3A, 3B, 5A, 2B, 1A, 4B, 1A, 2B, 5A, 2B) twice, 1B, 3A, 4B, 3A, 1[3]B.
These 2 rows establish the patt. Cont in patt working from chart, weaving the yarns into the back of the work, *at the same time* inc 1 st at each end of 15th chart row and on every foll 6th row until there are 100[104] sts.
Now work straight until 62nd row of chart has been completed.
**Shape armholes**
Keeping chart patt correct, cast off 5 sts at beg of next 2 rows, then dec 1 st at each end of foll 5 alt rows. 80[84] sts.
Now work straight until 110th row of chart has been completed.
**Shape shoulder and divide for neck**
**Next row** Cast off 8[10] sts, patt 25 sts including st used to cast off, cast off 14 sts, patt to end.
Work left side of neck first, leaving right side sts on spare needle.
**Next row** Cast off 8[10] sts, patt to end. 25 sts.
***Next row** Cast off 5 sts, patt to end. 20 sts.
**Next row** Cast off 8 sts, patt to end. 12 sts.
**Next row** Cast off 5 sts, patt to end.
Cast off rem 7 sts.
With ws facing rejoin yarn to right side neck edge. Complete to match left side from * to end.

LEFT FRONT
Using 4mm (US 6) needles and yarn A, cast on 42[44] sts.
Work in st st commence colour patt from chart working between left front markers, *at the same time* inc 1 at beg of 15th chart row and on every foll 6th row until there are 50[52] sts.

Damask Flower

1st row

2nd size | 1st size

1st size right front

1st size left front

1st size | 2nd size

1st size back

2nd size right front

2nd size left front

2nd size back

**Key**  □ = A  ☒ = B  ▣ = C

147

Flowers

Now work straight until 62nd row of chart has been completed.

**Shape armhole**
Cast off 5 sts at beg of next row and 1 st at armhole edge on foll 5 alt rows. 40[42] sts.
Now work straight until 93rd row of chart has been completed.

**Shape neck**
Cast off 4 sts at beg of next row, 3sts at beg of foll alt row, then 2 sts at beg of foll 3 alt rows. Now dec 1 st at beg of next 4 alt rows. 23[25] sts.

**Shape shoulder**
Cast off 8[10] sts at beg of next row and 8 sts at beg of foll alt row.
Work 1 row. Cast off rem 7 sts.

RIGHT FRONT
Work as given for left front, reversing all shapings and foll chart between right front markers.

SLEEVES
Using 3¼mm (US 3) needles and yarn A, cast on 46[50] sts.
Work 22 rows K1, P1 rib, in 1-, 2- and 3-row stripes, using yarns A, B and C as required.
Cont in rib stripes, inc 1 st at each end of next and every foll 6th row until there are 64[68] sts.
Change to 4mm (US 6) needles and cont in st st working chart patt between sleeve markers, *at the same time* shape sleeve by inc 1 st at each end of 5th and every foll 4th patt row until there are 84[92] sts on needle. Now inc 1 st at each end of every alt row until there are 104 sts on needle, ending with a P row and thus completing 62 chart rows in all.

**Shape top**
Cast off 5 sts at beg of next 2 rows, then dec 1 st at each end of next and foll 3 alt rows. 86 sts.
Now dec 1 st at each end of 8 foll 4th rows, then dec 1 st at each end of 6 foll alt rows. 58 sts.
**Next row** (P2 tog) to end. 29 sts.
Cast off.

LEFT FRONT BAND
Using 3¼mm (US 3) needles and yarn A, beg at neck edge, K up 84 sts down left front. P 1 row. K 3 rows to form foldline. Work 7 rows st st, beg with a P row.
Cast off loosely.

RIGHT FRONT BAND
Using 3¼mm (US 3) needles and yarn A, beg at lower edge, K up 84 sts, *at the same time* make buttonholes on K up row as foll:
**K up and buttonhole row** K up 2 sts, (K up 2 sts, lift 2nd st on right-hand needle over 1st st and off needle, K up 1 st, lift 2nd st on right-hand needle over 1st st and off, K up 8) 8 times, ending last rep K up 2.
**Next row** P to end, casting on 2 sts over those cast off in previous row.
K 2 rows to form foldline.
**Buttonhole row** K2, (cast off 2 sts, K 9 including st used to cast off) 7 times, cast off 2, K to end.
**Next row** P to end, casting on 2 sts over those cast off in previous row.
Work 6 rows st st, beg with a K row.
Cast off loosely.

TO MAKE UP
Backstitch shoulder seams. Backstitch sleeves into armholes, making three pleats either side of shoulder seam and matching patt across body and sleeve below pleats.
Backstitch side and sleeve seams.
Fold under front bands on foldlines and catch down lightly.

**Peplum**
Using 4mm (US 6) needles and yarn A, with rs facing K up 165[175] sts evenly around lower edge of jacket. Work in st st throughout.
**1st row** P5A, (5B, 5A) to end.
**2nd row** K5A, (5B, 5A) to end.
**3rd–4th rows** As 1st–2nd rows.
**5th row** As 1st row.
**6th row** K5A, (2B, K up loop between next st and last st to make 1, 3B, 2A, make 1, 3A) to last 10 sts, 2B, make 1, 3B, 5A. 196[208] sts.
**7th and 9th rows** P5A, (6B, 6A) to last 11 sts, 6B, 5A.
**8th row** K5A, (6B, 6A) to last 11 sts, 6B, 5A.
**10th row** K5A, (3B, make 1, 3B, 3A, make 1, 3A) to last 11 sts, 3B, make 1, 3B, 5A. 227[241] sts.
**11th–13th rows** Cont in st st using colours as set.
**14th row** K5A, (3B, make 1, 4B, 3A, make 1, 4A) to last 12 sts, 3B, make 1, 4B, 5A. 258[274] sts.
**15th–17th rows** Cont in st st, using colours as set.
**18th row** K5A, (4B, make 1, 4B, 4A, make 1, 4A) to last 13 sts, 4B, make 1, 4B, 5A. 289[307] sts.
**19th–21st rows** Cont in st st using colours as set.
**22nd row** K5A, (5B, make 1, 4B, 5A, make 1, 4A) to last 14 sts, 5B, make 1, 4B, 5A. 320[340] sts.
**23rd–29th rows** Cont in st st using colours as set.
Change to 3¼mm (US 3) needles.
Using yarn A, K 3 rows for foldline, then work 3 rows st st beg with a P row.
Cast off loosely.

**Peplum edging**
Using 3¼mm (US 3) needles and yarn A, with rs facing and beg at waist edge, K up 28 sts down left front of peplum.
K 2 rows to form foldline. Work 3 rows st st beg with a P row. Cast off.
Work a similar edging on right front peplum.
Fold peplum edgings under and catch down loosely.
Using 3.00mm (US D/3) crochet hook and yarn A, work a row of single crochet round neck edge.
Neaten buttonholes. Sew on buttons.

# T-shirt

A T-shirt shape is a useful basic shape on which to try out various designs. It's the same shape as the striped T-shirt on page 14 but worked from the bottom up instead of from side to side. I used it for another version of the Damask Flower design.

This time I used a mixture of thicker yarns (chenille, tweed, cotton, mohair and silk—some were combined to make up the thickness) and large needles. Because of this the scale of the flower motif is much bigger and it knits up more quickly than the peplum jacket.

The flower motif is charted in the same way as the one on the peplum jacket but here they are more widely spaced. The T-shirt is worked straight up, casting on for the sleeves, casting the centre stitches off and then on again for a slash neck, then working down the back in a mirror image of the front.

I used seven shades of mossy greens for the background, one being very bright, almost acid, and the others muted. The flower is in six very close shades of soft pink. The flower centres begin with bright turquoise, moving to powder blue and finishing with very pale green.

The main feature of this is the widely varying textures, giving a velvety brocade feel.

# Big Flower Jacket

Apart from the flower centres, there are only two colours to a row on this garment so it is very easy to knit. The background is simple stripes in different tones and the flower petals are all knitted in the same colour. Knit in all the ends as you go along and do try different colourways (see overleaf). On the whole I've kept the background colour fairly muted with the flowers being the brightest colours but it could be done the other way round—perhaps a highly coloured background with a black or grey flower.

MATERIALS
**Yarn used**
150g (6oz) Rowan Yarns Cotton Chenille in grey/green 361 (A); 100g (4oz) in driftwood 352 (C); 75g (3oz) in french mustard 363 (E); 50g (2oz) each in periwinkle 358 (D) and lavender 357 (B); 25g (1oz) in cloud blue 360 (F)
75g (3oz) Rowan Spun Tweed each in caper 762 (G) and iris 757 (J); 300g (11oz) in caviar 760 (H)
50g (2oz) Rowan Yarns Chunky Tweed in blue lovat 705 (L); 25g (1oz) in crimson pink 701 (M)
150g (6oz) Rowan Yarns Light Tweed in autumn 205 (N); 75g (3oz) in atlantic 223 (R); 50g (2oz) in jungle 212 (Q); 25g (1oz) each in pacific 221 (S), silver 208 (T) and scoured 201 (U)

# Damask Flower

25g (1oz) Rowan Yarns Fine Cotton Chenille in mole 380 (W)

75g (3oz) Rowan Yarns Double Knitting Wool in dark brownish red 71 (X)

**Equivalent yarn** chunky

1 pair each 5½mm (US 9) and 6½mm (US 10½) needles

8 buttons

## NOTE

*The finer yarns are used in combination. For example, 'HN' means one strand each of H and N; 'NQQ' means one strand of N and two of Q. If preferred chunky yarns used singly can be substituted for the combined yarns throughout.*

## TENSION

14 sts and 19 rows to 10cm (4in) over patt on 6½mm (US 10½) needles.

## MEASUREMENTS

**To fit bust/chest** 91–111cm (36–44in)

**Actual width** 129cm (50½in)

**Length to shoulder** 77cm (30in)

**Sleeve seam** 41cm (16in)

## BACK AND FRONTS (one piece)

Using 5½mm (US 9) needles and yarn M, cast on 72 sts.

Work in K1, P1 rib as foll: 1 row M, 11 rows HN.

**Next row** With HN, rib 2, K up st between next st and last st to make 1, (rib 4, make 1) to last 2 sts, rib 2. 90 sts.

*The idea of a huge dominating central theme is inspired by Japanese kimono designs. In particular, I like the way the Japanese split a motif down the middle, as I have done on the fronts of the jacket. The sage green flower colouring (far left) is the one specified in the pattern. The lavender and apricot flowers (below) are also knitted in chenille on a basically wool and mohair ground of neutral greys. I used silk in the flower centres. I also used silk in the Chinese pot in my needlepoint tapestry hanging behind them. I love the colour of this old, once pink door.*

## Flowers

Change to 6½mm (US 10½) needles and work in st st stripes, beg with a K row, foll colour sequence table for colour changes as foll: 2 rows in HN, 1 row in XX, 2 rows in E, 2 rows in NQQ and so on.

Work 52 rows in all in stripe patt, marking each end of 10th and 43rd rows for pockets, ending with a P row.

Commence flower patt working from chart, weaving yarns in at back of work, as foll:

**53rd row** (rs) K44HN, 2A, 44HN.
**54th row** P43C, 4A, 43C.

Cont as set working flower patt from chart and keeping stripe patt correct, foll colour sequence table for colour changes as before.

Work 55th–120th rows, marking each end of 74th row for sleeves.

Now cont in stripe patt only until 130 rows in all have been worked from top of rib.

**Divide for fronts**
**131st row** K41, cast off 8 sts, K to end.
**132nd row** P to neck edge, turn, leaving rem sts on a spare needle and cont on these sts only for left front. 41 sts.

**Shape back neck**
**133rd row** Cast off 4 sts, K to end. 37 sts.
**134th row** P to end.

The 134th row marks the shoulder line. (From this point foll colour sequence table in reverse from 134th–1st rows inclusive.)

Cont in reversed stripe patt, dec 1 st at beg of next row. 36 sts. Work 3 rows straight, thus ending at neck edge.

**Shape front neck**
Cast on 1 st at beg of next and 2 foll alt rows, then 2 sts at beg of foll alt row and 4 sts at beg of next alt row. 45 sts.

Now work straight until 121st row of colour sequence table has been worked, thus ending with a P row.

Commence flower patt reading left half of chart from top to bottom as foll:

**120th row** (rs) K3A, 42HN.
**119th row** P32HN, 6A, 3HN, 4A.

Cont as set working flower patt from chart and keeping reversed stripe sequence correct, work 118th–53rd rows, marking end of 74th row for sleeve.

Now cont in reversed stripe patt only, work 52nd to 1st rows, marking beg of 43rd row and end of 10th row for pocket.

Change to 5½mm (US 9) needles and cont in HN.
**Next row** (Rib 3, rib 2 tog) to end. 36 sts.
Work 11 rows K1, P1 rib.
Change to yarn M and rib 1 row. Cast off in M.

With ws facing, rejoin yarn to sts left on spare needle and work reversed stripe patt as for left front, reversing shapings, from 134th–121st rows inclusive, thus ending with a P row.

Commence flower patt reading right half of chart from top to bottom as foll:

**120th row** (rs) K42HN, 3A.
**119th row** P4A, 3HN, 6A, 32HN.

Cont as set working from chart and keeping reversed stripe sequence correct, work 118th–53rd rows, marking beg of 74th row for sleeve.

Cont in reversed stripe patt only, work 52nd–1st rows, marking end of 43rd row and beg of 10th row for pocket. Complete as for left front.

## SLEEVES

Using 5½mm (US 9) needles and yarn M, cast on 32 sts.

Work in K1, P1 rib as foll: 1 row M, 11 rows HN.

Change to 6½mm (US 10½) needles and work in stripe patt only as given for back and fronts, *at the same time* inc 1 st at each end of 3rd and every foll alt row until there are 90 sts.

Now work straight until 64th row of stripe patt has been worked.

Work 1 row in H.

Cast off loosely in H.

## RIGHT POCKET LINING

Using 6½mm (US 10½) needles and yarns HN, with rs of work facing, K up 26 sts between pocket markers on right back side edge.

P 1 row. Cont in st st, cast on 4 sts at beg of next row. 30 sts.

Now dec 1 st at beg of next and every foll alt row until 17 sts rem.

Cast off.

## LEFT POCKET LINING

K up sts on left back side edge as given for right pocket lining.

Work in st st, beg with a P row, cast on 4 sts at beg of 1st row, then dec 1 st at beg of next and every foll alt row until 17 sts rem.

Cast off.

## COLOUR SEQUENCE TABLE

| rows | ☐ | rows | ☐ |
|---|---|---|---|
| 1–2 | HN | 67–69 | GQ |
| 3 | XX | 70–71 | D |
| 4–5 | E | 72–74 | JR |
| 6–7 | NQQ | 75 | RRR |
| 8 | HQ | 76 | B |
| 9–10 | QXX | 77–79 | M |
| 11–13 | C | 80–81 | WX |
| 14 | JN | 82–85 | L |
| 15 | JR | 86 | F |
| 16 | RRR | 87–88 | JR |
| 17 | D | 89–94 | C |
| 18–19 | B | 95–96 | QW |
| 20 | JN | 97–100 | QQQ |
| 21–23 | RRR | 101–103 | NXX |
| 24 | F | 104–106 | B |
| 25 | L | 107–110 | HR |
| 26 | B | 111–112 | JR |
| 27–29 | NNR | 113 | C |
| 30–34 | C | 114–115 | GN |
| 35–38 | HN | 116–118 | D |
| 39–42 | HX | 119–120 | HN |
| 43–44 | QQX | 121 | QXX |
| 45–47 | E | 122–123 | E |
| 48–49 | L | 124–125 | NQQ |
| 50–53 | HN | 126 | JN |
| 54 | C | 127 | NRR |
| 55–60 | JN | 128 | RRR |
| 61 | NNR | 129 | D |
| 62 | E | 130–131 | B |
| 63 | L | 132 | JN |
| 64–66 | C | 133–134 | RRR |

POCKET EDGINGS (alike)
Using 5½mm (US 9) needles and yarn H, with rs of work facing, K up 26 sts between pocket markers on fronts.
K 1 row for foldline. Work 4 rows st st beg with a K row.
Cast off.

TO MAKE UP
Set sleeves in flat, matching centre of cast-off edge of sleeve to shoulder line and fitting between sleeve markers.
Press seams. Fold pocket edgings on to ws and catch down.
Backstitch side and sleeve seams. Catch down pocket linings on ws of fronts.
**Button band**
Using 5½mm (US 9) needles and yarns HN, with rs facing, K up 111 sts along right front edge (for a man's jacket, left front edge for a woman's).
P 1 row, then K 2 rows for foldline.
Change to yarn H and work 8 rows st st, beg with a K row.
Cast off loosely.
**Buttonhole band**
K up sts along second front edge as for button

band, *at the same time* make buttonholes on K up row as foll:
**K up and buttonhole row** K up 2 sts, (K up 2 sts, lift 2nd st on right-hand needle over 1st st and off needle, K up 1 st, lift 2nd st on right-hand needle over 1st st and off, K up 12) 8 times, ending last rep K up 1.
**Next row** P to end, casting on 2 sts over those cast off in previous row. 111 sts.
K 2 rows for foldline.
Change to yarn H.
**Next row** K2, (cast off 2 sts, K13 including st used to cast off) to last 4 sts, cast off 2 sts, K to end.
**Next row** P to end casting on sts over those cast off in previous row.
Work 6 rows st st, beg with a K row.
Cast off loosely.
Press front bands, fold on to ws of work along fold line and catch down.
**Collar**
Using 5½mm (US 9) needles and yarns HN, with rs facing, K up 64 sts evenly round neck edge.
Work 11 rows K1, P1 rib. Change to yarn M and rib 1 row.
Cast off in rib in M.
Neaten buttonholes. Sew on buttons.

*(Overleaf) To end, here are a few extravaganzas to whet your appetite for future projects: the huge red coat is an all-time favourite; two diagonal striped waistcoats inspired by carpets; the red jacket (also used as the background) was an ambitious early project; the waistcoat and jacket against a coloured brick wall employ the same geometric motif on different scales; finally, a detail of a large scarf on a Tibetan theme.*

Read this side of chart from top to bottom for left front, beg with a K row

Read this side of chart from top to bottom for right front, beg with a K row

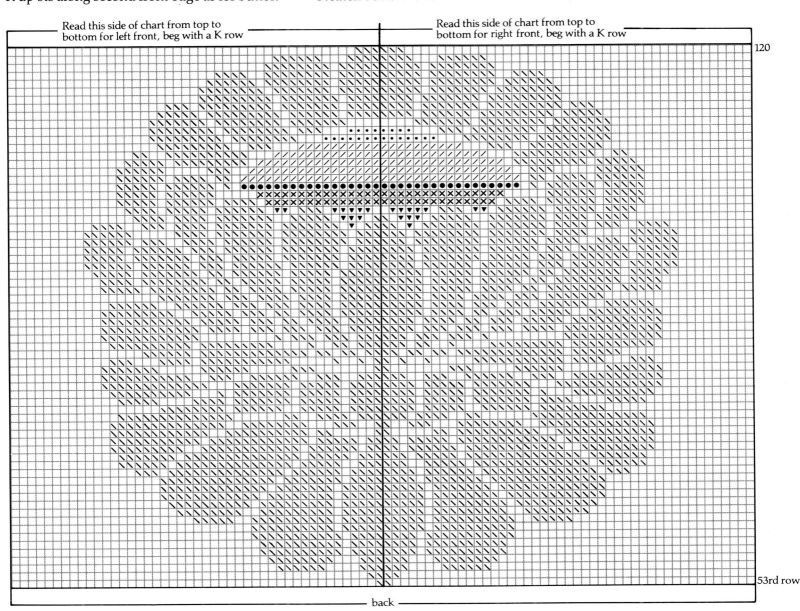

120

53rd row

back

**Key** ☐ background colour (see colour sequence table)   ◰ = A   ▼ = SSS   ⊠ = T   ▣ = STT   ⊘ = TTT   ⊡ = TUU